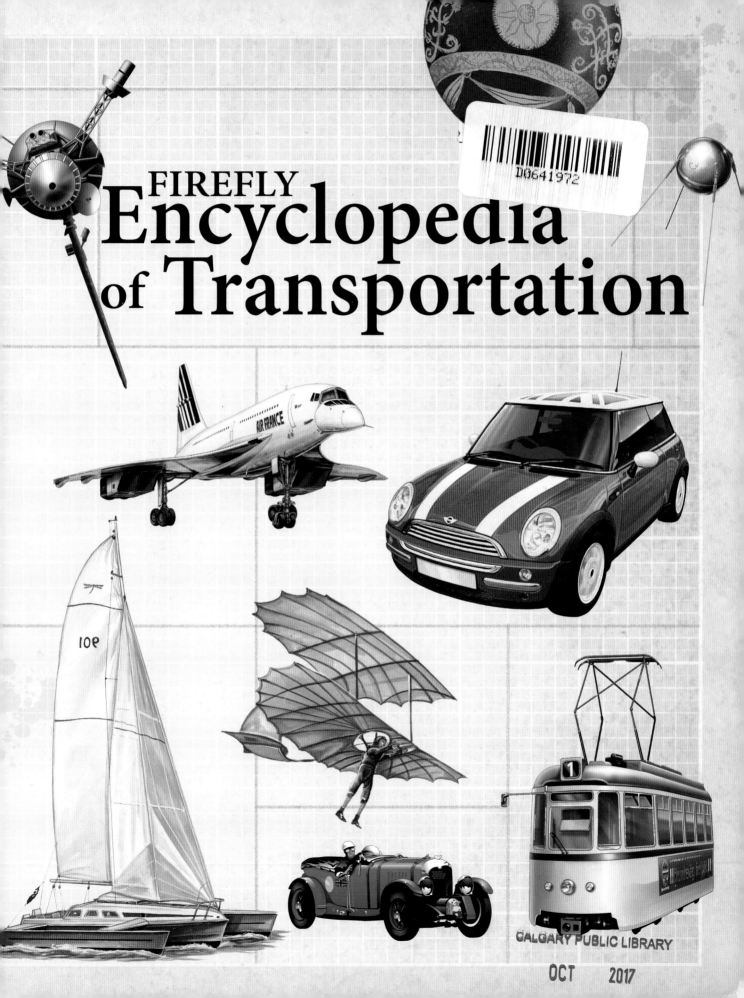

FIREFLY
Encyclopedia
of Transportation

A FIREFLY BOOK

Published by Firefly Books Ltd. 2017

First printing

Publisher Cataloging-in-Publication Data (U.S.)

Library of Congress Cataloging-in-Publication Data is available.

Library and Archives Canada Cataloguing in Publication

Green, Oliver, author
      Firefly encyclopedia of transportation : a comprehensive look at the world of
transportation / Oliver Green, Ian Graham, Philip Wilkinson, & Andrew Nahum.
Includes index.
ISBN 978-1-77085-931-9 (hardcover)
      1. Transportation--Encyclopedias, Juvenile. I. Graham, Ian, 1953-, author
II. Wilkinson, Philip, 1955-, author III. Nahum, Andrew, author IV. Title.
V. Title: Transportation encyclopedia.
 TA1149.G74 2017   j388.03   C2017-900443-3

Published in the United States by
Firefly Books (U.S.) Inc.
P.O. Box 1338, Ellicott Station
Buffalo, New York 14205

Published in Canada by
Firefly Books Ltd.
50 Staples Avenue, Unit 1
Richmond Hill, Ontario L4B
0A7

Printed in China

General Consultants: Oliver Green,
Research Fellow and former Head
Curator, London Transport Museum;
Andrew Nahum, Senior Curator,
Aeronautics and Road Transport,
Science Museum, London

Contributors: Philip Wilkinson, Ian
Graham, Oliver Green, Howard
Johnston, Ian Ward

Consultants: Tracks: Tim Bryan,
Steam: Museum of the Great Western
Railway, Swindon; Water: Pieter van
der Merwe, General Editor, National
Maritime Museum, Greenwich; Space:
Douglas Millard, Associate Curator,
Space Technology, Science Museum,
London

FIREFLY
Encyclopedia
of Transportation

A comprehensive look at the world of transportation

Oliver Green, Ian Graham,
Philip Wilkinson & Andrew Nahum

FIREFLY BOOKS

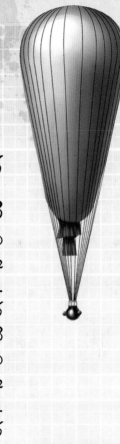

CONTENTS

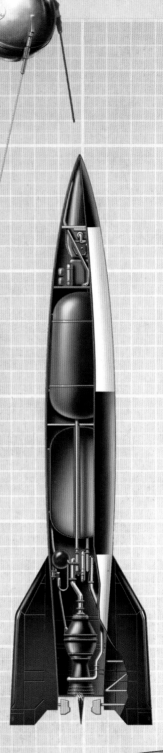

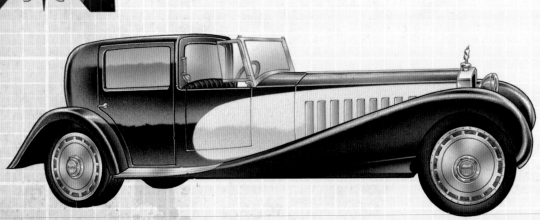

INTRODUCTION

Since the earliest times, people have traveled — to find food, to carry goods for trading, or for sheer adventure — to find out what is over the next hill or to find new lands across the sea. To begin with, they walked or rode animals, but they built the first boats in prehistoric times, and wheeled vehicles were first used 5,000 years ago.

For thousands of years, these forms of transportation developed gradually. Boat-builders designed better sails and methods of steering their craft; different styles of cart and carriage were developed for land transportation. These changes came slowly, but they had a huge effect. For example, better ships enabled people such as the Vikings to go on the first long-distance voyages of exploration, crossing the Atlantic in search of new places to settle. Again in the 15th and 16th centuries, European explorers used the latest ships to go huge distances, some even sailing right around the globe. But few people traveled that far. Most men and women did not go far beyond their immediate neighborhood, and if they did travel long distances, the journey was likely to be slow, difficult, and dangerous.

Then, in the 19th century, a change took place which transformed transportation for good. Engineers in Europe developed the railways, bringing fast, safe land transportation within the reach of many people for the first time.

The railways also allowed goods to be transported faster and more efficiently than ever before, helping industry and making people less reliant on food and other items produced near home.

Rapid transport, rapid change

By the beginning of the 20th century, the next leap forward in the story of transportation had taken place. The first cars were on the road and the first airplanes were in the air. Suddenly, the world seemed a smaller place and the pace of change got faster. Cars became cheaper and better designed; aircraft grew in size and got faster; ocean liners became more luxurious and cargo vessels got bigger. In every area of transportation, engines were made both more powerful and more efficient and there were improvements in comfort and safety.

Today in the developed world, many families own at least one car and regular air travel is a reality. It seemed that people could travel anywhere they wanted, but in 1961 the Russians amazed the world by sending the first person into space.

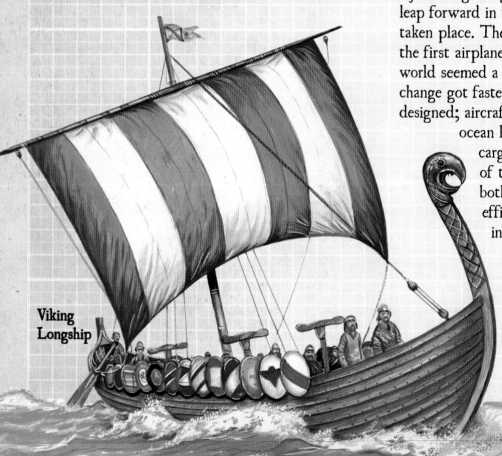

Viking
Longship

By the end of the 1960s, men had walked on the moon and in the next decade unmanned space probes were sent far out into the solar system. Nearer the ground, the supersonic airliner Concorde had cut down the journey time between London and New York to a mere three hours.

Traveling in the future

In the future, transportation on the ground and at sea may also become much swifter, with faster trains, cars, and ships on the drawing board. But governments and manufacturers are trying to make transportation more efficient, so that we use less of the world's precious resources as we travel around. There are already exciting experimental boats and cars powered by the sun's rays, and many scientists hope that the fuel cell, already used in some spacecraft, will one day provide quiet, efficient, low energy power for many other vehicles. Meanwhile, designers are always coming up with ways of making cars, trains, boats, and planes more streamlined, to cut down drag and get more speed with less fuel. The resulting vehicles perform better, and often look amazing too.

HOW TO USE THIS BOOK

This book is divided into six easy-to-follow sections, dealing with transportation on the road, on railways, in the water, in the air, in space, and greener transportation. Within each section, most of the pages contain a series of catalog-style entries on a range of craft and vehicles. Each entry contains the story of the vehicle and a fact box to see, at a glance, aspects from speed and size to the number of people carried. In addition, each section contains feature pages that focus on particular topics, such as Formula One racing, high-speed trains, or around-the-world balloons. Finally, at the back of the book you will find fact-packed lists on famous people, amazing transportation facts, what the technical terms mean, and a timeline of transportation history.

ON WHEELS

Long before the invention of the automobile, there was plenty of road transportation — chariots, stagecoaches, Hansom cabs and other vehicles. Bumpy roads made long journeys uncomfortable, but they were possible. Even the simple bicycle was a big help in getting people around.

When the automobile was invented at the end of the 19th century people tried to ban it or to control its speed so it was slower than a horse. Early laws even required someone to walk ahead waving a red flag. In 1908, the first mass-produced car, the American Model T Ford, opened up the prospect of cheap transportation for everyone. By 1922, there were 2 million Model Ts alone, and by the year 2000, 35 million cars were being produced each year.

From wooden cartwheels to massive monster truck tires, the wheel is one of humankind's most important inventions.

The very first Ford car (above, right) and the 10 millionth Ford (above, left), in 1924. In over a century of car manufacture, Ford has designed many different models of car, and sold more than 350 million.

The Fiat 500 was the first "mini-car" to seat four people. Its small size made it the perfect vehicle for towns and cities.

Fiat 500, 1957

Station Wagon   **Hatchback**   **Sports**   **Convertible**

What is a car?

The wheel was invented over 5,000 years ago, but the car has only been around for just over 100 years. How would we manage now without this handy form of transportation that has gone from being a crude horseless carriage to a high-tech machine? Along with the building of road systems, the car has literally changed our planet.

Parts of a car

Nearly all cars have four wheels, each one with a spring to absorb the bumps. The engine is usually at the front, mounted sideways and driving the front wheels only. Bodies are steel, aluminum or plastic.

Tire types

Tires are round and usually black. Standard tires have some grooves to clear water away, but off-road versions are very knobby, to grip better in mud. Old tires were very narrow and had little grip.

Car types

Sedans are standard cars, minivans take larger families. Station wagons carry lots of luggage, while hatchbacks have an opening tailgate and folding rear seats. Convertibles can be sports or sedans. Compact cars are for the city, 4×4s go anywhere.

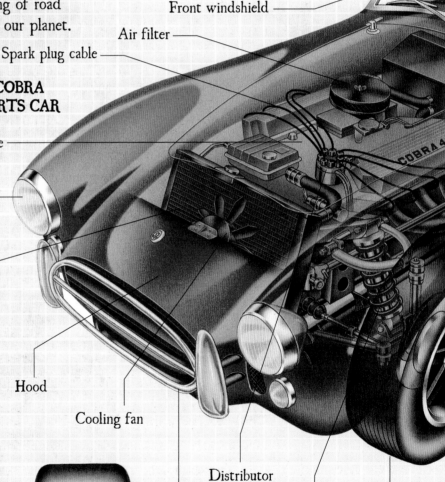

AC COBRA SPORTS CAR

Front windshield —

Air filter —

Spark plug cable —

Engine —

Headlight —

Radiator —

Hood —

Cooling fan —

Distributor —

Bumper —

Shock absorber inside coil spring —

Front tire —

Early solid rubber

Early air-filled

Standard grooves

Racing (no grooves)

Compact

Off road

Stretched

Minivan

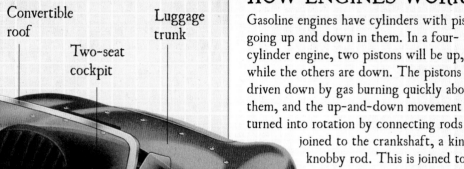

Convertible roof

Two-seat cockpit

Luggage trunk

Brake disc

Steering wheel

Steering column

Exhaust pipe

HOW ENGINES WORK

Gasoline engines have cylinders with pistons going up and down in them. In a four-cylinder engine, two pistons will be up, while the others are down. The pistons are driven down by gas burning quickly above them, and the up-and-down movement is turned into rotation by connecting rods joined to the crankshaft, a kind of knobby rod. This is joined to the wheels of the car by the clutch and the gearbox.

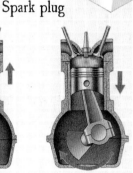
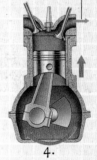

Cylinder

Valves

Camshaft

Piston

Crankshaft

Connecting rod

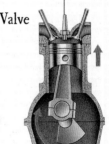

Fuel and air mixture

Spark plug

Exhaust

Valve

Piston

1.   2.   3.   4.

The four-stroke cycle

Most engines run on the four-stroke or Otto cycle. As a piston moves down the cylinder, a valve opens to allow a fuel and air mixture to be sucked in. As the piston starts to rise again, the valve closes and the mixture is squeezed. Near the top of the piston stroke, a spark plug lights the mixture, which burns quickly and expands to push the piston down again. Near the bottom once more, another valve opens to allow the rising piston to force the waste "exhaust" gas out. Then the cycle starts again.

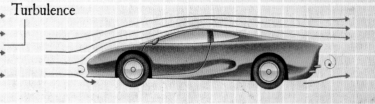

Turbulence

Aerodynamics (airflow)

What looks streamlined usually is, but wind tunnels have allowed car designers to make smoother shapes with low "drag," which means more speed for less fuel.

In a boxy old-fashioned sedan, the flow of air over the body is not smooth, because of the angles. In a sleek sports car, there are fewer turbulent areas to create drag.

Before engines

Once people discovered how to roll rather than slide things, transportation became much easier. By 3000 BC, domesticated animals were harnessed to pull carts, the designs of which were to improve over the centuries. There were experiments using sails and even clockwork motors, but oxen were the most common.

Country: Italy
Date: c. 200 BC
Size: 13¼ ft (4.2 m) long
Body: wood
Top speed: 15 mph (24 km/h)
On board: 1 or 2

Roman chariot

Chariots were pulled by two, three or four horses, and the one or two passengers used to stand. The Roman army used chariots to transport spear carriers and archers. Fighting chariots even had sharp blades attached to the wheels. Chariot racing was very popular.

Country: Europe
Date: 1100s
Size: 10 ft (3 m) long
Body: wood
Top speed: 3 mph (5 km/h)
On board: 0

Oxen farm cart

After the invention of the wheel (see page 48), sleighs were modified into simple carts. In the 1100s, these carts were used for farm work, with oxen to pull them. Each cart could carry much more produce at one time than ever before.

Chinese wheelbarrow

Wheelbarrows were first used in China around 200 AD. They were different from modern garden barrows because they had the load over the wheel rather than behind it, which made them easier to lift. Some barrows even had sails to help them along.

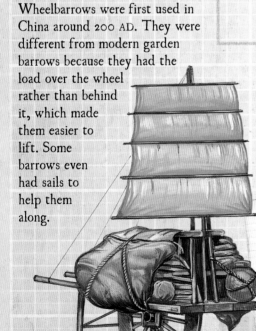

Country: Europe
Date: 1600s
Size: 11 ft (3.4 m) long
Body: wood
Top speed: 11¼ mph (2 km/h)
On board: 2

Country: China
Date: c. 200 AD
Size: 5 ft (1.5 m) long
Body: wood with fabric sail
Top speed: 2½ mph (4 km/h)
On board: 0

Treadmill

One of many attempts at replacing animals to pull carts was this self-propelled carriage. It was steered by rope, and power came from the man at the back "walking" on a tread wheel that made the rear axle turn. In fact it would have been easier to push the vehicle along, and the vehicle was a failure.

Country: UK
Date: 1834
Size: 6 ft (1.8 m) long
Body: wooden body and wheels, with iron tires
Top speed: 6 ½ mph (10 km/h)
On board: 2 plus driver

Hansom cab

John Hansom invented this light and elegant two-wheeled cab. It was a common sight in Victorian London. The driver sat high up at the back and on top of the cab, and he could talk to his passengers through a trapdoor in the roof. There was a folding door at the front and a bench seat above the two wheels.

Stagecoach

By 1802, Americans could travel the 1,200 miles (1,900 km) from Boston to Savannah in "stages" by different coaches. The best known stagecoach was the Concorde, of which nearly 4,000 were made. They carried passengers inside with a driver and guard on top with the luggage. Leather springs made the ride more comfortable, with greater speed given by six horses.

Country: U.S.
Date: 1830
Size: 12 ft (3.7 m) long
Body: wood with leather springs, metal strengthening
Top speed: 15 mph (24 km/h)
On board: 6 plus 2 crew

Covered wagon

Canvas-covered wagons were the caravans or trailers of the 1850s. Some 55,000 U.S. settlers used them to head west, often in groups called wagon trains. The wooden frames could carry several tons, and were usually hauled by oxen or mules — often in teams of six — and could only manage about 20 miles (30 km) a day.

Country: U.S.
Date: 1850s
Size: 12 ft (3.7 m) long
Body: wood
Top speed: 3¾ mph (6 km/h)
On board: 2 or 3

The first cars

During the Industrial Revolution, horse and carriage slowly became "horseless" carriage thanks to the invention of the steam engine, which powered the first cars. In the 1870s and 1880s, Karl Benz and Gottlieb Daimler developed the first crude gas-engined buggies. They were slow and unreliable and many of them looked like carts without the horse, but soon cars began to appear with a front-engine rear-wheel drive that became the basis of modern transportation.

Country: France
Date: 1878
Size: 13 ft (4 m) long
Body: wood and steel
Top speed: 6½ mph (10 km/h)
On board: 6 plus firearm at rear

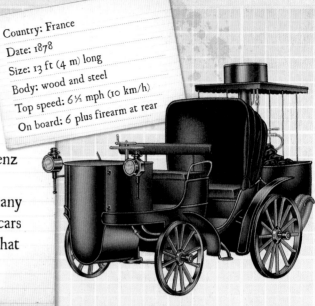

La Mancelle

Amédée Bollée's La Mancelle steamer set the style for automobiles to come. It might look crude but it featured a front-mounted engine driving the rear wheels, and a simple linkage steering. Though not fast, La Mancelle (meaning "The Girl from Le Mans") did run down a horse in Paris, France.

Country: Germany
Date: 1885/86
Size: 8 ft (2.5 m) long
Body: wood and steel
Top speed: 9 mph (15 km/h)
On board: 2

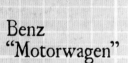

Benz "Motorwagen"

The first workable car, named after its inventor Karl Benz, was a three-wheeled vehicle with a tubular steel frame and an open wooden two-seater body. The single front wheel was steered by a tiller, while the two larger rear wheels were driven by chains. The gas engine was mounted crossways between the rear wheels.

Country: Germany
Date: 1886
Size: 8 ft (2.5 m) long
Body: wood and steel
Top speed: 15 mph (25 km/h)
On board: 2

Benz Viktoria

The Viktoria was the first four-wheeler from Karl Benz, one of the most famous names in the motor industry. It was also the first car to carry a model name, the first car to have an accurate steering system, and the first car to go into proper production. The Viktoria appeared in 1893 and still looked as though it had lost its horses, but at least it had a steering wheel of sorts, rather than a tiller.

Panhard-Levassor

Early French carmakers Panhard-Levassor rolled out their first car in 1891. By 1895, they had created the modern car blueprint — four wheels, a front-mounted engine, gearbox in the middle, and rear-wheel drive.

Country: France
Date: 1894
Size: 8 ft (2.5 m) long
Body: wood and steel
Top speed: 12½ mph (20 km/h)
On board: 4

Country: U.S.
Date: 1910
Size: 11½ ft (3.5 m) long
Body: steel and wood
Top speed: 55 mph (88 km/h)
On board: 4

Oldsmobile Curved Dash

Named after the shape of the footboard at the front, the Curved Dash was the world's first mass production car. A factory fire destroyed all the drawings, but the prototype survived, so many thousands of copies were still made from 1901 to 1905. The engine was under the seats and the little runabout was speedy, which must have been quite scary with tiller steering.

Country: U.S.
Date: 1901
Size: 8 ft (2.5 m) long
Body: wood and steel
Top speed: 20 mph (32 km/h)
On board: 2

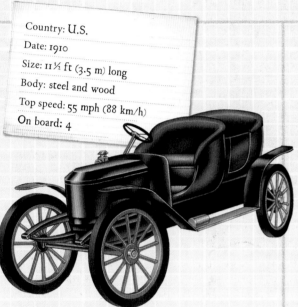

Stanley Model 71

Although gas quickly became the favorite fuel for those early cars of the 1880s, steam power was favored by the U.S. Stanley company right into the 1920s. This 20hp tourer was typical, with its boiler mounted under the front hood and the engine at the back driving the rear wheels. It was a speedy motor.

Renault

With its engine in the front under a proper hood, driving the rear wheels, this 1899 vehicle actually looked like a car, rather than a buggy that had lost its horses. Drivers needed goggles because there was no windshield and night driving was dangerous with only oil lamps to light the way. In 1900, Renault sold 179 cars.

Country: France
Date: 1899
Size: 10 ft (3 m) long
Body: wood and steel
Top speed: 12½ mph (20 km/h)
On board: 4

Mean machines

There are some wheeled vehicles that stand out from the crowd. They are bigger, heavier, taller, longer, or faster than anything else. Some may have been "customized" — like hot-rod cars "sunk" low and fitted with extra wide wheels and a powerful racing-tuned engine, or "stretched limos" with extra chassis and wheels to allow passengers to stretch out and enjoy television, a refrigerator, and a bar. Some are built for sport, others to carry important people safely with bullet- and bomb-proofing, and some to beat a speed or endurance record.

Bigfoot

Bigfoot began as a pick-up truck with big tires and suspension for car crushing displays at fairs. The tires are over 6 ft (1.8 m) high. Bigfoots (or monster trucks) have powerful engines and lightweight bodies to set long jump records of over 200 ft (62 m).

Country: U.S.
Date: 1976
Size: 18 ft (5.5 m) long
Body: alloys on a tubular frame
Top speed: 65 ½ mph (100 km/h)
On board: 2

AEC Mammoth Major

This 1960s "road-train" was specially built in Australia by the British AEC company. It could carry 110 tons (100 tonnes) of goods at a time across the vast Australian outback (where there are no railways). Throwing up clouds of dust, it resembled a fast-moving crocodile in the sand.

Country: Australia
Date: 1960
Size: 148 ft (45 m) long with 3 trailers
Body: steel and alloys
Top speed: 55 mph (88 km/h)
On board: 3

Thrust SSC

This was the first car to break the sound barrier, at Black Rock Desert, Nevada, in July 1997. Driven by Andy Green, it took just 4.67 seconds to pass through the measured mile. At the record speed, the big aluminum wheels rotate 8,500 times a minute and the parachutes released to slow down the vehicle give 11 tons (10 tonnes) of braking force.

Country: UK
Date: 1997
Size: 47 ¾ ft (14.6 m) long
Body: steel frame, aluminum panels
Top speed: 763 mph (1221 km/h)
On board: 1

Dragster

This dragster's huge engine is tuned to produce 6,000 horsepower for the four seconds it takes to pass through a measured mile. The front steering wheels are tiny, but the back tires are huge because they have to drive the dragster. The driver sits just behind the engine, which is cooled by ice and runs on an alcohol-based fuel.

Country: U.S.
Date: 2000
Size: 19 ¾ ft (6 m) long
Body: steel frame, some composite paneling
Top speed: 200 mph (320 km/h)
On board: 1

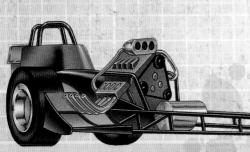

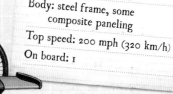

Peterbilt truck

With their chrome exhaust stacks pointing to the sky, such huge "long-nosed" or hooded trucks haul loads of more than 44 tons (40 tonnes) across America. These massive transporters are built to travel millions of miles in their lifetime.

Country: U.S.

Date: 1990s

Size: 40 ft (12.2 m) long

Body: steel frame with aluminum cab

Top speed: 60 mph (96 km/h)

On board: 2 or 3

Panoz AIV Roadster

Looking like a 1950s hot rod, the Panoz has a powerful V8 engine delivering 305 horsepower. It can go from 0 to 60 mph (0–100 km/h) in 4.6 seconds. Each car takes 350 hours to hand-build and many of the parts are developed from racecars.

Country: U.S.

Date: 1990

Size: about 13 ft (4 m) long

Body: AIV (aluminum intensive vehicle) frame and panels

Top speed: 143 mph (230 km/h)

On board: 2

Hummer HMMWV

The powerful Hummer began life as a go-anywhere vehicle for the U.S. army. The initials HMMWV stand for High Mobility Multi-Purpose Wheeled Vehicle, often shortened to Humvee. A civilian version was first marketed by General Motors in 1998. It can climb up incredibly steep hills and go through up to 5 ft (1.5 m) of water but its huge size and poor fuel economy with a gas engine made it impractical as an everyday vehicle. The last Hummer was built in 2010.

Country: U.S.

Date: 1982

Size: 15 ft (4.6 m) long

Body: steel and alloys

Top speed: 80 mph (128 km/h)

On board: up to 10

Luxury cars

All the first cars were hand-built from the finest timbers and hand-painted with the fully upholstered seats, carpets and curtains reflecting the luxury of horse-drawn carriages before them. The 1920s saw the coachmaker's craft at its peak, with royalty and movie stars demanding leather seats, walnut dashboards, and even gold or silver plating. The luxury car market continues today with high-quality stereos and space-age navigation systems.

Bugatti 41 Royale

The stuff that legends are made of, the Bugatti Royale was so large that a Mini could be parked on its hood. Only six examples were sold. The engines later found use in high-speed French railcars.

Country: France
Date: 1926
Size: 22 ft (6.7 m) long
Body: steel
Top speed: 100 mph (160 km/h)
On board: 6

Country: France
Date: 1930
Size: from 16 ft (4.8 m) long
Body: steel
Top speed: 100 mph (160 km/h)
On board: 2 to 6 depending on body style

Delage D8

Built during the golden age of luxury automobiles, the Delage D8 came in various styles to suit most people — as long as they were wealthy. The sporting D8S and D8SS models could manage well over 100 mph (160 km/h). Unfortunately, the years leading up to World War II in 1939 saw wealth declining, and the D8 took Delage into bankruptcy and a takeover by Delahaye.

Hispano-Suiza H6 B

Designed by Swiss engineer Mark Birkigt, this was from 1919 to 1938 the most technically advanced car in the world. Its six-cylinder engine was a masterpiece and its four-wheel brakes (themselves unusual) were power-assisted, which was unheard of.

Country: France
Date: 1919
Size: 16 ft (4.8 m) long
Body: steel
Top speed: 85 mph (137 km/h)
On board: 2 to 6 depending on body style

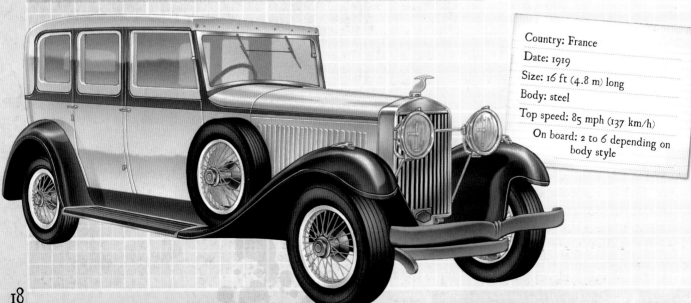

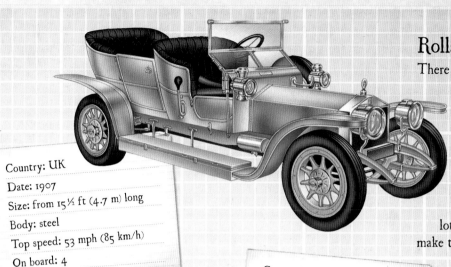

Rolls-Royce Silver Ghost

There is actually only one Silver Ghost, although there were, and are, many Rolls-Royce type 40/50s. That unique car has silver-plated fittings and still belongs to Rolls-Royce. It was taken on a series of reliability trials including running from London to Edinburgh in top gear. This did a lot to stake the Rolls-Royce claim to make the best car in the world.

Country: UK

Date: 1907

Size: from 15½ ft (4.7 m) long

Body: steel

Top speed: 53 mph (85 km/h)

On board: 4

Mercedes S-Class

With a sleeker body than before, this top-of-the-range "Merc" had just about every possible accessory, together with all kinds of electronic wizardry, such as rain-sensing windshield wipers, and electric seats with built-in memory.

Country: U.S.

Date: 1974

Size: 20 ft (6 m) long

Body: steel

Top speed: 120 mph (192 km/h)

On board: 6

Country: Germany

Date: 1999

Size: 16.6 ft (5.1 m) long

Body: steel

Top speed: from 145 mph (232 km/h)

On board: 5

Lincoln Town Car

Lincoln is still the Ford motor company's American luxury brand. It started as an independent company in the 1920s and was named after the founder's hero, President Abraham Lincoln. This 1970s Town Car had a distinctive coffin-shaped hood and retractable headlights. Its great size was typical of American sedans of the time, as was the "gas-guzzling" 7.5-liter V8 engine.

Country: Japan

Date: 1998

Size: 16¼ ft (5 m) long

Body: steel

Top speed: 143 mph (230 km/h)

On board: 5

Lexus GS300

Lexus is the name coined by Toyota for its luxury range of cars. The GS300 has a powerful six-cylinder engine and was one of the first cars to have a built-in satellite navigation system with voice instructions to guide the driver to his or her destination. A GPS (global positioning system) has since become a standard feature of most medium-sized cars.

People movers

The earliest cars could often seat four people, but the price was too high for the average family. It was only when Henry Ford put his famous Model T into mass (factory) production that family motoring became a real possibility. Since then this type of car, with plenty of seats and doors, has been the most popular, with many manufacturers competing hard to win sales. Today, minivans have become very popular, particularly for larger families, but medium-sized sedans are as much in demand as ever.

Bullnose Morris Cowley/Oxford

"Bullnose" comes from the shape of the radiator. Cowley, in Oxford, was the place of manufacture. Between 1913 and 1926, more than 150,000 of the two cut-price cars were built.

Country: UK

Date: 1913

Size: 12 ft (3.7 m) long

Body: steel

Top speed: 50 mph (80 km/h)

On board: 2 to 4 depending on body style

Model T Ford

"Any color as long as it's black" was one of the sayings for which car maker Henry Ford was famous. It applied to his Model T Ford, which introduced machine-made cars for the masses for the first time. Between 1908 and 1927, more than 15 million Model Ts were made. Such was the speed of production that there was no time to paint cars different colors at first.

Country: U.S.

Date: 1908

Size: from 11½ ft (3.5 m) long

Body: steel

Top speed: 45 mph (72 km/h)

On board: 2 to 4 depending on body style

Volkswagen Beetle

This simple but innovative car, with its air-cooled engine, was designed by Dr. Ferdinand Porsche (who later designed the famous Porsches). He was responding to a German government demand for a Volkswagen (meaning "people's car"). From a shaky start in World War II, around 20 million cars were built.

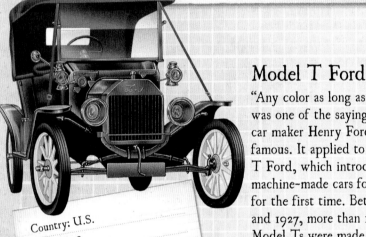

Country: Germany

Date: 1939

Size: 13.1 ft (4 m) long

Body: steel

Top speed: 60 mph (100 km/h) depending on model

On board: 4

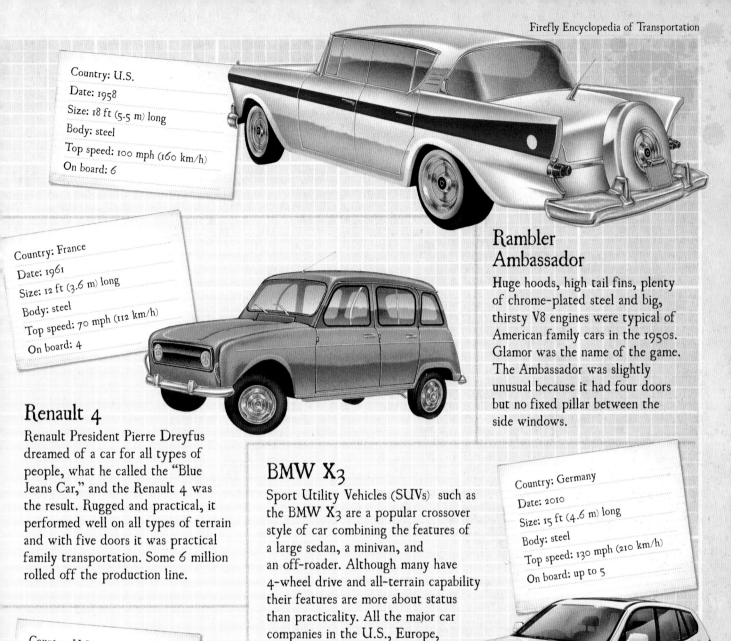

Country: U.S.

Date: 1958

Size: 18 ft (5.5 m) long

Body: steel

Top speed: 100 mph (160 km/h)

On board: 6

Rambler Ambassador

Huge hoods, high tail fins, plenty of chrome-plated steel and big, thirsty V8 engines were typical of American family cars in the 1950s. Glamor was the name of the game. The Ambassador was slightly unusual because it had four doors but no fixed pillar between the side windows.

Country: France

Date: 1961

Size: 12 ft (3.6 m) long

Body: steel

Top speed: 70 mph (112 km/h)

On board: 4

Renault 4

Renault President Pierre Dreyfus dreamed of a car for all types of people, what he called the "Blue Jeans Car," and the Renault 4 was the result. Rugged and practical, it performed well on all types of terrain and with five doors it was practical family transportation. Some 6 million rolled off the production line.

BMW X3

Sport Utility Vehicles (SUVs) such as the BMW X3 are a popular crossover style of car combining the features of a large sedan, a minivan, and an off-roader. Although many have 4-wheel drive and all-terrain capability their features are more about status than practicality. All the major car companies in the U.S., Europe, Japan, and China now produce a range of SUV models.

Country: Germany

Date: 2010

Size: 15 ft (4.6 m) long

Body: steel

Top speed: 130 mph (210 km/h)

On board: up to 5

Country: U.S.

Date: 2000

Size: 15.4 ft (4.7 m) long

Body: steel

Top speed: 109 mph (175 km/h)

On board: up to 7

Chrysler Voyager

As a multi-purpose vehicle, or MPV, the Chrysler Voyager was intended to provide the space of a minivan and the comfort of a luxury car. Features include chairs that swivel to face each other, and sliding doors on each side to give plenty of room to get in and out.

Compact cars

Small cars are cheaper to buy than larger versions. They use less fuel and so cost less to run, and their size makes them ideal for busy city streets. Many models, such as the Renault 5 and Volkswagen Golf have appealed across all class and age barriers to attract a kind of cult following. In reality, small cars do not cost much less to make than their bigger brothers and Austin-Morris famously lost money on the legendary Mini for many years.

Austin Seven

One of the most famous cars of all, the Austin Seven set a new style for mass motoring during its 16-year life. Sturdier than the fragile cycle-cars of the day, it was very affordable, with many versions, from tiny two-seaters to graceful sedans.

Country: UK
Date: 1923
Size: 8¾ ft (2.7 m) long
Body: steel
Top speed: 40 mph (64 km/h)
On board: 2 to 4 depending on body style

Country: France
Date: 1948
Size: from 12½ ft (3.8 m) long
Body: steel
Top speed: from 35 mph (55 km/h)
On board: 4

Heinkel/Trojan 200

The "bubble car" appeared in the dull 1950s. These zippy three-wheelers were produced by famous German aircraft manufacturers — and one was the Heinkel. It was later manufactured in Britain as the Trojan. Powered by a tiny rear engine, it had a single front door but could still house two people in comfort and more in a pinch. They continued into the 1960s, until the Mini put an end to this particular fashion.

Citroën 2CV

"Four wheels under an umbrella" was the brief to the designer of the 2CV, which also had to be capable of crossing a field without breaking one of a load of eggs. Designed in the 1930s, but held back by World War II, it had a tiny air-cooled engine, lift-off doors, fold-back roof and removable hammock seats. By 1984, 5 million had been sold.

Country: Germany/UK
Date: 1956
Size: 7¾ ft (2.4 m) long
Body: steel
Top speed: 55 mph (88 km/h)
On board: 2

Country: Italy
Date: 1957
Size: 9 ft (2.7 m) long
Body: steel
Top speed: 60 mph (96 km/h)
On board: 2 to 4

Fiat 500

The Fiat 500 was the first true mini-car. Although its 500 cc twin-cylinder engine was hidden behind the back seat, the car had a proper hood and could carry four people — slowly! Known in Italy as the Cinquecento, this tiny machine was a slow seller at first, but by the time it gave way to the Fiat 126 in the 1970s, more than 3 million 500s had been sold.

Austin/Morris Mini

At a time when most cars had dull designs, Alec Issigonis's Mini was revolutionary. This tiny car had good interior space thanks to an engine fitted sideways. In its Mini Cooper form, it had great racing success.

Country: UK
Date: 1959
Size: 10 ft (3 m) long
Body: steel
Top speed: from 72 mph (115 km/h)
On board: 4

Country: UK, Germany
Date: 2001
Size: 11½ ft (3.6 m) long
Body: steel
Top speed: 130 mph (210 km/h)
On board: 4

BMW Mini Cooper

The new Mini launched by BMW in 2001 has no connection with Issigonis's original other than the name. It is not as small and compact as the first Mini, but the stylish retro design cleverly suggests the spirit of the original brought up to date for the 21st century. It is now a very popular and successful model with a growing range of variations and is still built in Oxford, England using robot technology in a new factory on the site of the original Mini plant.

Ford Ka

Ford's smallest car quickly became a popular and successful runabout. It originally had a striking body shape based entirely on rounded curves. This unique styling led to the Ka being selected for display at the Museum of Modern Art (MoMA) in New York even though it was not sold in the United States.

Country: Europe
Date: 1996
Size: 11¾ ft (3.6 m) long
Body: steel
Top speed: 96 mph (155 km/h)
On board: 4

Country: Japan
Date: 1999
Size: 11¾ ft (3.6 m) long
Body: steel
Top speed: 96 mph (154 km/h) depending on model
On board: 4

Toyota Yaris

Toyota's baby hatchback was acclaimed as European Car of the Year 2000. An apparently new concept saw the designers figuring out what interior space was needed for comfort and then building the car around that. This gave a tall yet compact car, with good seating for four.

Sports cars

Sports cars are designed to accelerate from 0 to 60 mph (0 to 100 km/h) in just a few seconds, and some can reach speeds of up to 185 mph (300 km/h). Even though such speeds are well over legal road limits, people love the thrill of handling such powerful machines, especially compared with family sedans, which are heavier, slower and less responsive to fast turning or accelerating. Typical sports cars are two-seaters with a soft-top roof that can be folded down.

BMW Z3

Built first in the U.S. for Americans, this little German sports car quickly became popular in Europe too. It is a traditional sports car, with only two seats and a front 3.2-liter engine driving the rear wheels. The Z3 also comes with an electrically operated hood.

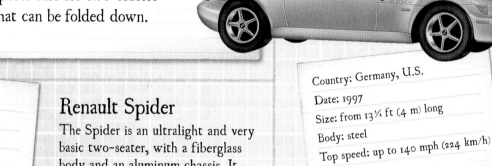

Country: Germany, U.S.

Date: 1997

Size: from 13 ¼ ft (4 m) long

Body: steel

Top speed: up to 140 mph (224 km/h)

On board: 2

Country: France

Date: 1997

Size: 12 ½ ft (3.8 m) long

Body: fiberglass

Top speed: 135 mph (214 km/h)

On board: 2

Renault Spider

The Spider is an ultralight and very basic two-seater, with a fiberglass body and an aluminum chassis. It is unlike anything else that Renault has made. Just behind the seats is the 2.0-liter engine, which drives the rear wheels and gives the Spider great stability when cornering.

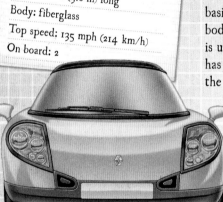

Country: Germany

Date: 1964

Size: from 12 ¼ ft (4.3 m) long

Body: steel

Top speed: 181 mph (290 km/h) in turbo versions

On board: 2

Jaguar XK-SS

This was a roadgoing version of the Le Mans 24-hour racecars, the 1950s D-type Jaguars. Only 16 cars were completed before fire destroyed the factory where they were built. Those few cars are very valuable today, and the curved design of the XK-SS was developed into the world-famous E-type Jaguar.

Country: UK

Date: 1957

Size: from 14 ¼ ft (4.3 m) long

Body: steel

Top speed: 149 mph (240 km/h)

On board: 2

Porsche 911

The 911 was first made in 1964 and continued until 1997 without changing its sleek, aerodynamic shape. All models had their air-cooled engines mounted behind the rear wheels, and they required care when cornering at speed.

Alfa Romeo Montreal

Italian carmakers Alfa Romeo have produced world-beating racing and touring cars since the 1920s. Named after the Canadian city where it was first shown, the coupé Montreal was powered by a version of the V8 engine that was also in Alfa Romeo's successful Tipo 33 racecars of the 1960s and 1970s.

Country: Italy

Date: 1970

Size: from 13 ft (4.2 m) long

Body: steel

Top speed: 137 mph (220 km/h)

On board: 2 + 2

Aston Martin DBR2

The DB series of Aston Martins were named after David Brown, who once owned the company. The DBR2 was a very smooth and sleek sports racecar. Its very powerful 3.7-liter engine helped it win the Le Mans 24-hour race and the World Sports Car Championship in 1959.

Country: UK

Date: 1957

Size: 13¾ ft (4.2 m) long

Body: steel

Top speed: 175 mph (280 km/h)

On board: 2

Country: U.S.

Date: 1953

Size: from 13 ft (4 m) long

Body: fiberglass

Top speed: about 100 mph (160 km/h)

On board: 2

Chevrolet Corvette

For many years the Corvette was the best known American sports car, and the first to be mass-produced with a fiberglass body. They are still made today but they look nothing like those early models, which have since become highly sought-after collectibles.

Ferrari 250 GTO

Only 39 of the 250 GTOs were built, and this is one of the most sought-after cars today. Its sleek coupé bodywork was developed after wind tunnel tests at Pisa University, which, in the early 1960s, was still unusual. With a mighty V12 engine, the GTO could reach over 160 mph (260 km/h).

Country: Italy

Date: 1962

Size: 14½ ft (4.4 m) long

Body: steel

Top speed: 165 mph (266 km/h)

On board: 4

Off-road vehicles

The first off-road car was the General Purpose vehicle, shortened to GP, and nicknamed "Jeep." It became famous during World War II (1939–45) when different models and sizes carried the U.S. army almost anywhere. Its powerful engine, four-wheel drive (previous cars were two-wheel drive only), and large, deep-tread tires enabled troops to go through desert, ice, mud and other difficult terrain. After the war, people began using Jeeps and cars like them for fun and exploring. Today's Jeeps are much more comfortable, with leather seats and air-conditioning.

Willys Jeep

The Jeep was built by a number of companies during World War II to a standard design approved by the U.S. Army, but it was Willys who registered the name in 1945. Very basic, it was also rugged and surprisingly fast. 635,000 examples were made before peace came.

Country: U.S.

Date: 1940

Size: 11 ft (3.3 m) long

Body: steel

Top speed: 70 mph (113 km/h)

On board: 4

Land Rover

With a steel frame and aluminum body panels, early models had three "bucket"-shaped seats up front, and one even featured a central steering wheel. By 1976, one million had been sold worldwide to farmers, the police and the army for working in rough and slippery conditions. The last traditional Land Rover Defender rolled off the production line in 2016.

Country: UK

Date: 1948

Size: 13 ft (4 m) long

Body: aluminum alloy

Top speed: 85 mph (136 km/h)

On board: 2 to 9

Country: UK

Date: 1970

Size: 14 ¾ ft (4.5 m) long

Body: aluminum and steel

Top speed: 100 mph (160 km/h)

On board: 5

Mercedes M Class

The German Mercedes M Class is built for the American market. It has leather seats, air-conditioning, four airbags and an on-board computer. Special suspension and insulation make it even more comfortable on rough ground. It can also go through 2 ft (0.5 m) of water without flooding.

Range Rover

The large and comfortable Range Rover was designed as an all-terrain vehicle (ATV) to handle normal city streets or difficult muddy forest tracks. With a big V8 engine driving all four wheels, it was also powerful. It could pull itself up steep hills or through the muddiest terrain.

Country: Germany, U.S.

Date: 1998

Size: 15 ft (4.6 m) long

Body: steel

Top speed: 112 mph (180 km/h)

On board: 5 to 7

Country: U.S.
Date: 1998
Size: 12 ¾ ft (3.9 m) long
Body: steel
Top speed: 92 mph (147 km/h)
On board: 4

Jeep Wrangler

This modern open-top Jeep is fun and safe. It comes equipped with safety features such as airbags, all-steel doors, a skid plate under the fuel tank and a gearbox case to protect the underside of the vehicle. Four-wheel drive can be selected on the move if needed suddenly.

Toyota Land Cruiser

Launched as a basic but rugged all-terrain vehicle, the Land Cruiser has sold in vast numbers worldwide. Today, it is made in two luxury versions, the Colorado and the Amazon. There is an on-board compass, an inclinometer to tell you how steep a track is and even an altitude display. This is an SUV with the roadholding stability of a four-wheel drive.

Country: Japan
Date: 2000
Size: 14 ft (4.3 m) long
Body: steel
Top speed: 100 mph (160 km/h)
On board: 8

Country: U.S.
Date: 2000
Size: 15 ¾ ft (4.8 m) long
Body: steel
Top speed: 100 mph (160 km/h)
On board: 5

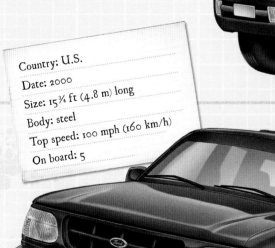

Ford Explorer

A long-standing favorite here in the U.S., the Explorer was not introduced to Europe until 1997, but it is now a top-selling off-road vehicle all over the world. It features a big engine, selectable four-wheel drive and automatic transmission (clutch and gearbox) to help it through tough terrain. It is also well equipped for family driving. Air-conditioning, electric windows, mirrors, sliding roof and seats, cruise control and an electronic compass are some of the on-board items.

Autosports

Since the earliest days of driving, there have been motor races: the French Grand Prix dates back to 1906. At that time, racecars were huge machines capable of 90 mph (145 km/h). Today's racecars can comfortably reach 200 mph (320 km/h). But not all racing takes place on a racetrack. Rallying is almost like off-road racing, often on dirt tracks, where the driver relies on sideways spins to corner, the opposite of circuit racing, in which smooth turning drivers are the quickest.

Country: various
Date: 1992
Size: 6 ft (1.8 m) long
Body: steel tube frame and seat
Top speed: 150 mph (240 km/h)
On board: 1

Zip Kart

This kart is light enough to be picked up by one person. It is made up of a tube frame with a seat, a steering wheel, pedals and a small engine at the back. Because it is so small, it can "zip" around Grand Prix circuits at 150 mph (240 km/h), and its tiny tires are wide enough to allow the kart to go around corners very fast. Less powerful 25-mph (40-km/h) versions are popular at go-kart tracks.

Ford Focus

This rally version of a standard Focus has extra body strength and special suspension. The engine produces more than twice as much power as the standard road car, so it can go at very high speeds on rough, windy tracks, often through thick forests. When they are rallying, the driver and his navigator talk to each other through an intercom in their helmets because it is so noisy.

Country: UK
Date: 2000
Size: 13¼ ft (4.2 m) long
Body: Reinforced steel and carbon fiber
Top speed: 150 mph (240 km/h)
On board: 2

Country: France
Date: 1999
Size: 15 ft (4.6 m) long
Body: steel and composites
Top speed: 112 mph (180 km/h)
On board: 2

Schlesser Renault Buggy

Jean-Louis Schlesser's Buggy is strengthened and has special springs to tackle the tough desert surfaces on the 6,250-mile (10,000 km) Paris–Dakar Rally (Europe to Africa). The engine is from a Renault Megane road car, but it is highly modified for extra power.

Daf SRT-II

A turbo-charged engine helps this racing truck accelerate fast enough to leave most sports cars behind. The cab is strengthened, leaving room for only a driver, and the truck is so light that more weight has to be put on to load it down.

Country: Netherlands
Date: 1998
Size: 14 ¾ ft (4.5 m)
Body: steel and lightweight composites
Top speed: 112 mph (180 km/h)
On board: 1

Country: Germany
Date: 2000
Size: 15 ft (4.6 m) long
Body: carbon fiber
Top speed: 200 mph (320 km/h)
On board: 1 (officially 2)

Audi/Le Mans

Audis are not usually associated with the famous Le Mans 24-hour race, but in 2000 an aerodynamic racing Audi won the event. It is built of lightweight materials, such as carbon fiber, and its engine, which sits behind the driver, can power it to speeds of well over 185 mph (300 km/h).

Ford Taurus

This Ford won the 1999 Daytona 500, which is the most famous NASCAR (National Association for Stock Car Auto Racing) event. It looks like a standard "stock" or sedan car that customers can buy, but in fact it has been altered to speed along banked oval circuits in some 30 U.S. races each year.

Country: U.S.
Date: 1999
Size: 16 ft (5 m) long
Body: Lightweight alloys
Top speed: 200 mph (320 km/h)
On board: 1

Reynard 961

Like many Indy cars racing on the American road and oval race circuits, the Reynard is built in the UK. Though they look like Formula One racers (see pages 30–31), average lap speeds of these U.S. racing cars are 232 mph (373 km/h), and they run on alcohol fuel, not gasoline. A gear change takes 16 milliseconds, and a gearbox copes in two hours with what a road car suffers in a lifetime.

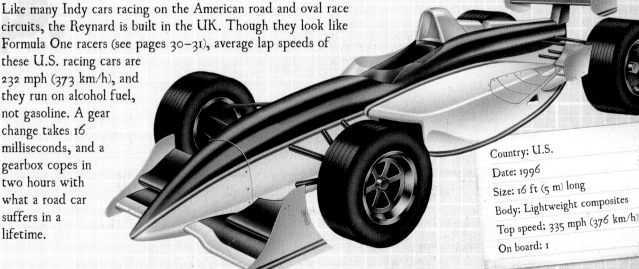

Country: U.S.
Date: 1996
Size: 16 ft (5 m) long
Body: Lightweight composites
Top speed: 335 mph (376 km/h)
On board: 1

1914

1930

1939

Formula One cars

Formula One cars are the fastest — reaching speeds of 200 mph (320 km/h) — and the drivers are the most skilled in the world. There is only room for one person, who sits in front of the engine. The wheels are uncovered and the tires are very wide to grip the road well. Wings are used at the front and back to press the cars down and help them to go around corners fast. The wings give so much downward force at high speed that the cars could drive along a ceiling upside down without falling off.

The pit crew

A large team of people look after each car at a Grand Prix race. They work very fast during the race, changing four tires and filling the fuel tank in less than 10 seconds.

Protective clothing

Every driver wears a crash helmet to protect his head in a crash and a special suit to help prevent injury if a fire starts after an accident. The suit is made of several layers of special fireproof fabric.

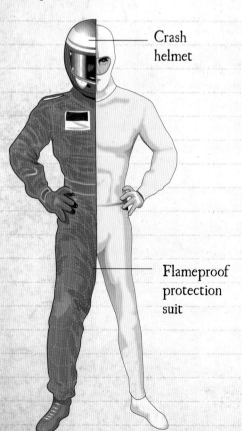

Crash helmet

Flameproof protection suit

Racecars

Racing and sports cars have changed a great deal since the early 1900s, when cars used to carry riding mechanics. Some early racers had huge engines, which made them very fast, but they were heavy and their tires were narrow, so the grip on corners was poor. The modern design, with the engine just behind the driver, and the car as low as 35 in. (90 cm) began in the 1960s.

F1 CAR DESIGN

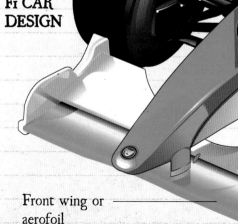

Front wing or aerofoil

1950   **1963**   **1970**

The race flags

Officials at race meetings still use flags to get messages to drivers, though most communications are electronic and the cars have radios.

 Yellow flag shows that there is danger ahead, such as an accident.

 Red flag shows that a race has been stopped.

Blue flag shows that a faster car is coming up, usually to lap a driver.

White flag warns there is a slow moving vehicle ahead (i.e. an ambulance).

Green flag shows that the track is clear, particularly after yellows.

Black flag with a car's number on it indicates that the car must stop.

 Checkered flag is waved at the finish line, when the winner passes.

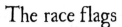 **Yellow and red flag** warns that the track ahead is unusually slippery.

Gearbox

Air inlet

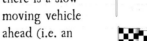

Rear wings or aerofoils for downward force

Rear tire

Engine

Cockpit

 Bathtub chassis

Front suspension

Front wheel

Racing circuits

Most of the circuits used for Grand Prix are specially built, but one of the oldest, in the Principality of Monaco, is on ordinary roads, with safety barriers put up for the race. Because this circuit is narrow and twisty, it is slow, but others, such as Hockenheim in Germany, have long straights that allow the cars to go very fast.

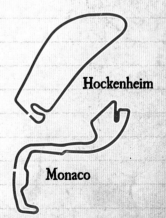

Hockenheim

Monaco

War-zone vehicles

The first military vehicles were the wheeled siege towers and battering rams used by the Assyrians of Asia in the 9th century BC. Leonardo da Vinci drew a battle car in 1484, and in 1855 James Cowen invented an armed, wheeled, armored vehicle based on the steam tractor. World War I (1914–18), saw real mechanized warfare with the first steel-plated tanks. They moved on metal chains called tracks, and today are armed with powerful cannons on revolving turrets.

Country: UK
Date: 1916
Size: 26½ ft (8.1 m) long
Body: armored steel plates
Top speed: 3¾ mph (6 km/h)
On board: 8

Vickers tank

Tanks were first made with caterpillar tracks to cross mud, trenches and barbed wire during World War I. They were called "tanks" to conceal their real purpose from the enemy. The "male" Vickers had cannons on the side and the "female" had machine guns. Their first battle was the Somme in 1916. Inside they were very hot, noisy and uncomfortable.

AC armored car

This gunless armored car, made by AC, was one of the first produced. It had an ordinary car frame, with thick steel body work to protect the crew. The driver looked ahead through a small slit in the front and even the radiator had armored doors. However, the wheels could easily be damaged and the tires punctured in action.

Country: UK
Date: 1914
Size: 12 ft (3.7 m) long
Body: Heavy steel
Top speed: 31 mph (50 km/h)
On board: 6

Country: Germany
Date: 1940
Size: 12½ ft (3.8 m) long
Body: steel
Top speed: 56 mph (90 km/h)
On board: 4

DUKW

DUKWs were nicknamed "Ducks" because they could travel over water from ship to shore at 6¼ mph (10 km/h). All the wheels steered, and helped the rudder in water. About 1,000 DUKWs took part in the invasion of Sicily (1943).

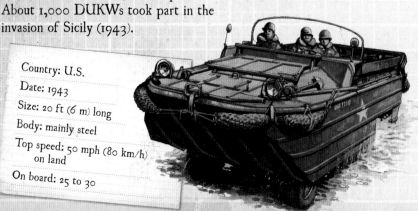

Country: U.S.
Date: 1943
Size: 20 ft (6 m) long
Body: mainly steel
Top speed: 50 mph (80 km/h) on land
On board: 25 to 30

Kubelwagen

The Kubelwagen was the German army's version of the VW Beetle (see page 20). It was designed by Dr. Porsche and during World War II (1939–45) more than 50,000 were built. It did not have four-wheel drive, like the Jeep (see page 24), but with very simple mechanical parts, it was reliable. It was used to carry soldiers in battle areas, and there was even an amphibious version called the Schwimmwagen.

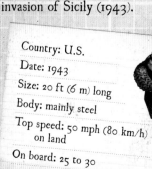

White M3A1 Scout Car

This was a popular command vehicle. It had four-wheel drive to cope with any terrain. Though it was armored and carried a machine gun, passengers were still exposed to enemy fire. Some were used as ambulances or to transport mechanics.

Country: U.S.

Date: 1940

Size: 18 ft (5 m) long

Body: armored steel

Top speed: 55 mph (88 km/h)

On board: up to 12

Sherman M4A3

More than 48,000 Sherman tanks were built during World War II (1939–45). With its welded "turtle-backed" hull and central cast turret supporting a 76-mm gun, it proved very reliable as an Allied tank during the war. However, it fell behind the gun power and standard diesel engine of the German tanks. Some were still in use in South America in the 1990s.

Country: U.S.

Date: 1941

Size: 20 ft (6.3 m) plus long gun barrel

Body: steel frame and armor

Top speed: 30 mph (48 km/h)

On board: 5

Leopard 2 tank

Weighing 65 tons (59 tonnes), this is one of the toughest tanks in the world. The Leopard 2 has very thick armor and separate protection for the crew compartment. Its main gun is a 5-in. (120-mm) cannon, which can be kept steady even when the tank is bouncing, and it carries 42 shells for this. It has a very powerful diesel engine, and is specially armored on the hull and turret. Over 2,000 of these German tanks have been made.

Country: Germany

Date: 1979

Size: 25¼ ft (7.7 m) long

Body: steel frame with armor

Top speed: 45 mph (72 km/h)

On board: 4

Farm vehicles

Until the late 19th century, there was hardly anything mechanical on the farm. Almost all agricultural work was still done by hand, with horses or oxen used to pull equipment like ploughs and farm wagons. Steam power was introduced for a few heavy tasks but mechanical tractors only appeared gradually in the 20th century. Large-scale mechanized farming with tractors and combine harvesters began in the U.S. but was not widespread in Europe until the 1960s. Today moving machines are an essential part of farming nearly everywhere.

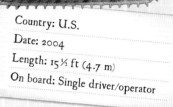

Country: U.S.
Date: 2004
Length: 15 ½ ft (4.7 m)
On board: Single driver/operator

Allchin traction engine

A traction engine is a self-propelled steam engine that could be used to move heavy loads by road off the railway. It was also used to bring a mobile power source to farms and other locations before electrical generators were available. With the traction engine stationary, the large raised flywheel could be used with a belt to drive other machines such as fairground rides by steam. Farmers could hire traveling agricultural engines that worked in pairs winching a plow to and fro across a field or powering early threshing machines at harvest time.

Country: UK
Date: 1910
Engine power: 7 hp
On board: crew of two

Caterpillar D8 crawler tractor

Crawler tractors move on tracks like tanks and are useful for working on rough and uneven ground, especially in mud and snow. They are slow, but the steel tracks spread the weight evenly, giving these all-terrain vehicles excellent grip and stability. First introduced in 1935, the powerful D8 Caterpillar has been in production for over 70 years. It can be used to haul farm equipment but is normally supplied with a large detachable front blade and rear ripper for use as a bulldozer on demolition and construction sites.

Country: U.S.
Date: 1917
Size: 102 in. (2.6 m)
Engine power: 20 hp
On board: single driver

Fordson Model F tractor

The Fordson Model F was the first lightweight tractor to be cheaply mass-produced like the Ford Model T automobile. It revolutionized agriculture by enabling farmers to replace horses on many tasks with an affordable and reliable machine. A farmer with a tractor could plant and raise crops over a much larger area than before and increase production with fewer workers. Fordsons and similar tractors were soon being built at factories in the U.S., Europe and the Soviet Union.

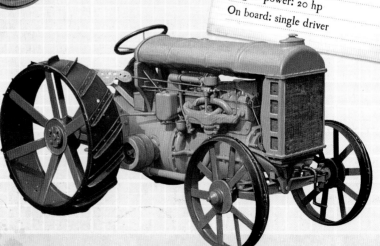

Country: Japan/U.S.

Date: 2006

Length: 75 in. (190 cm)

On board: single driver

Honda FourTrax 350 ATV

Small all terrain vehicles (ATVs), also known as quad bikes or four wheelers, were first developed in the 1980s. The rider sits on and operates an ATV like a motorcycle, with the two extra wheels giving greater stability at lower speeds. ATVs are popular for off-road sport and recreational activities and are extensively used in agriculture where rapid access to remote sites on rough ground may be needed, such as sheep farming and forestry.

Country: U.S.

Date: 2013

Length: 16.4 ft (5 m)

Lift height: 12.3 ft (3.75 m)

On board: single driver/operator

Massey Ferguson tractor/loader

Tractors now come in a wide range of sizes and can be fitted with mounted or towed equipment both front and back. This Massey Ferguson model has a removable loader with hydraulic rams that help to lift heavy loads in the bucket. It can be controlled by the driver using a joystick inside the cab to make the bucket tip and pivot. The tractor can also carry sprayers, mowers, seed drills and other specialty attachments. Tractors have become versatile machines with multiple uses well beyond the farm.

Claas Lexion 570 combine harvester

A combine is a machine that harvests grain crops and combines three separate operations — reaping, threshing and winnowing — into a single process. It is one of the most important labor-saving inventions used in agriculture, first developed in Australia in the 1880s with horse-drawn machines. Self-propelled combines with engines were developed in the U.S. in the 1920s. Today Claas is the largest European manufacturer of combines. On-board electronics and flexible cutting heads allow a wide range of different crops to be harvested efficiently with these sophisticated machines.

Country: Germany

Date: 1995

Engine power: 448 hp

On board: single driver/operator

Trucks

The earliest trucks used gasoline engines or steam power, but in the 1920s the German Benz Company introduced diesel-powered trucks. Diesel engines were more powerful and enabled trucks to travel farther on a single tank of fuel. Modern trucks are either "rigid" (having a single and straight chassis frame), or "articulated" (jointed) with two parts: a tractor unit that carries the engine, cab and driving wheels, and a detachable trailer.

De Dion Bouton

Even in the early 1920s, some trucks were purpose-built to perform special tasks. This De Dion Bouton road-sweeper had a brush that turned as the truck moved and collected roadside trash. The dirt was then sucked into the bag on the back of the truck. The rest of the truck was old-fashioned with open cabin sides and cart-type wheels.

Country: France

Date: 1922

Size: 16½ ft (5 m) long

Body: wood and steel

Top speed: 20 mph (32 km/h)

On board: 2

Scammel Scarab

The Scarab could turn around in small spaces, because of a clever pivot between the cab and the trailer, the pointed nose and the single front wheel. It was ideal for stations, where one tractor could handle several trailers.

Country: UK

Date: 1949

Size: 29½ ft (9 m) long

Body: steel (later fiberglass cab)

Top speed: 30 mph (48 km/h)

On board: 2

Vabis 1.7-ton truck

One of the first Swedish trucks, this Vabis had a simple platform on a steel girder frame. The tiny engine at the front drove the back wheels. There were springs, but the ride was not comfortable for the exposed driver.

Country: Sweden

Date: 1903

Size: 15 ft (4.5 m) long

Body: wood and steel with wooden wheels and steel tires

Top speed: 12½ mph (20 km/h)

On board: 2

CAT 621E scraper

These huge machines are often seen alongside big new roads being built. Even the tires are taller than a person. These machines can scrape up to 13 in. (33 cm) of earth at a time to level the surface, and carry nearly 24 tons (22 tonnes) of soil. The scraper is on a swiveling link to the tractor at the front, and both parts have a powerful diesel engine.

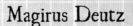

Country: Germany

Date: 1980

Size: 24 ¼ ft (7.4 m) long

Body: steel

Top speed: 50 mph (80 km/h)

On board: 3

Magirus Deutz

This "tipper" has two wheels on each end of both back axles to help with carrying very heavy loads of sand and gravel. The whole of the load container can be tipped by an engine-powered ram. With the back panel unfastened, it can be unloaded in a few seconds.

Diamond T tanker

Quite unlike any other gasoline tanker, this truck had its tank carefully merged into the cab to create a streamlined "railway engine" look. It also had no separate chassis (frame), so all its strength came from its bodywork. The engine was at the back so the driver could sit ahead of the front wheels.

Country: U.S.

Date: 1934

Size: 33 ft (10 m) long

Body: steel

Top speed: 56 mph (90 km/h)

On board: 2

Country: U.S.

Date: 1989

Size: 42 ft (12.9 m) long

Body: steel

Top speed: 30 mph (50 km/h)

On board: 1

Buses

The first "omnibuses" were large horse-drawn coaches used on fixed routes in major cities from the 1820s, including Paris, London and New York. It was the start of urban public transportation. The name, meaning "for all" in Latin, was originally painted on the side of the vehicle, and was later shortened to "bus." Gas-engined motor buses appeared in the 1900s and were very unreliable at first, but had replaced most city horse buses in Europe and the U.S. by 1914. Today, long-distance coaches come with individual lighting, air-conditioning, toilets and reclining seats.

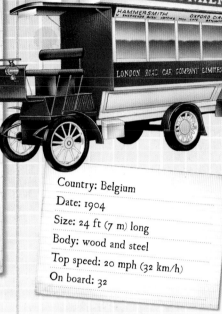

Country: Belgium
Date: 1904
Size: 24 ft (7 m) long
Body: wood and steel
Top speed: 20 mph (32 km/h)
On board: 32

Country: UK
Date: 1930
Size: 19½ ft (6 m) long
Body: aluminum and wood
Top speed: 46¾ mph (75 km/h)
On board: 18

Bean single deck

By today's standards the Bean's engine was not powerful, and it took up a lot of room. With the driver and the door behind him, there was even less room for passengers. If the engine stopped, the driver might have to resort to restarting the bus by winding the handle hanging from the front.

Germain open top

Early buses, like this Germain, were built on a truck chassis. This one, which was used in London, had its driver sitting on the hood to leave as much room as possible for passengers. An outside staircase led to the roof. People would have a good view from there, but would get wet if it rained. The ride was slow and bumpy and the buses often broke down.

Sunbeam trolley bus

Trolley buses have electric motors. They pick up electricity through "trollers" (arms) on the roof that run along overhead wires. They do not run on rails as trams do. On this double-decker version, the stairs to the top deck were at the back and a conductor collected the fares while on the move. Sometimes, the arms would come off the wires and the driver would use a special long pole to push them back up.

Country: U.S., Canada
Date: 1948
Size: 34½ ft (10.5 m) long
Body: wood and steel
Top speed: 53 mph (85 km/h)
On board: 33

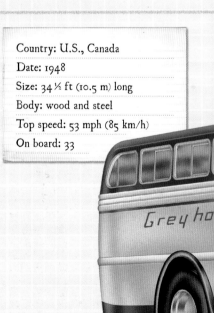

Country: UK
Date: 1946
Size: 32¾ ft (10 m) long
Body: steel
Top speed: 40 mph (64 km/h)
On board: 66

Berliet PCM bus

In the UK, city buses are often high-capacity double deckers, but single deckers are the norm in European and American cities. This Berliet is typical of the buses used in Paris and other French cities in the 1960s, with folding air doors at the front, center and back all controlled by the driver. It has a diesel engine at the front, but most modern buses now have it mounted under the seats at the back.

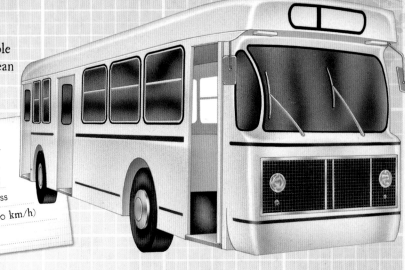

Country: France

Date: 1968

Size: 32¾ ft (10 m) long

Body: steel and fiberglass

Top speed: 62 mph (100 km/h)

On board: 40

AmTran school bus

American school buses are made by many different companies, but they are always yellow and easy to spot. This one has a high floor with low doors for ease of access. Multiple mirrors allow the driver to make sure it is safe to drive off, and flashing lights on the top warn other drivers.

Country: U.S.

Date: 1999

Size: 31¼ ft (9.5 m) long

Body: welded steel

Top speed: 65 mph (105 km/h)

On board: 54

MCI courier

This single-decker coach was the standard inter-city passenger bus in the U.S. and Canada in the late 1940s and early 1950s. The American Greyhound Line covers vast distances, so comfort is important. This was one of the first buses to have reclining seats. The high floor meant that passengers had a good view and that luggage could be stowed in a compartment below.

Pedal power

Most modern bicycles are still based on designs over 150 years old. The first pedal cycle was the velocipe of 1865, built by Michaux in France. It was very heavy and the thick iron tires made the ride very bumpy, leading to the nickname "boneshaker." Today, some bikes are so light they can be lifted with just a finger. Human powered vehicles (HPVs) are also pedal-powered, but the riders recline in a bucket seat and steer with a joystick.

Penny-farthing

The earliest bicycles had the pedals working directly on the front wheels. This meant that a bigger wheel made the bike travel farther for each turn, so the wheels grew bigger (and the back wheel smaller) until some were 5 ft (1.5 m) across. This was the ordinary bicycle of 1872, better known as the penny-farthing because it resembled two coins of the day.

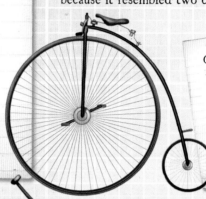

Country: UK, U.S., France
Date: 1872
Size: 5 ft (1.5 m) long
Body: steel frame and spoked wheels, with leather saddle
Propulsion: pedals on front wheel

Country: France
Date: 1816
Size: 6 ft (1.8 m) long
Body: iron frame and wheels, with leather saddle
Propulsion: feet on ground

Dandy horse

Also called the "hobby horse," this bicycle had two spoked wheels in line joined by a frame, just like a modern bike, but it had no pedals. Instead, the rider walked while sitting astride the machine to speeds of 9½ mph (15 km/h).

Raleigh Superbe

Touring bikes such as the Raleigh Superbe were made in the 1950s as the demand for cycles for leisure travelers and commuters increased. Its simple three-speed gear system made climbing hills easier, the chain had a cover to keep grease off clothes and there were mudguards and lights.

Country: UK
Date: 1949
Size: 6 ft (1.8 m) long
Body: tubular steel frame with leather saddle and steel mudguards
Propulsion: chain drive from pedals, with gears

Country: UK
Date: 1886
Size: 5¾ ft (1.7 m) long
Body: tubular steel frame with rubber tires and leather saddle
Propulsion: chain drive from pedals

Starley's Safety 1886

This bicycle looked very much like a modern bicycle with equal-sized wheels. It featured a rear wheel driven by a large chain wheel on the pedals, and a small chain wheel on the rear wheel, giving it gears. The tires were solid rubber and the bike shook a lot, but it made cycling much more popular, taking the place of the penny-farthing.

Marin Mount Vision

This lightweight mountain bike was the first with suspension on both front and rear wheels to win a major cross-country championship. The knobby tires are tough and give extra grip on loose surfaces. The bike's tubing is made of aircraft-quality aluminum.

Country: U.S.
Date: 1999
Size: 5½ ft (1.6 m) long
Body: lightweight aluminum frame with full suspension
Propulsion: chain drive with 21 gears

Brompton folding bike

The original Brompton folding city bike was designed by Andrew Ritchie in 1975. It has small wheels, a lightweight frame and a unique, easy-to-use folding system. Folding down a Brompton takes less than 20 seconds, creating a compact package that can easily be taken on a train or stowed inside an office, making it a popular choice for commuting. Bromptons are custom made in west London, with 80 percent of them exported around the world.

Country: UK
Date: 1988 (volume production)
Folded length: 23 in. (0.59 m)
Body: steel (or customized titanium/aluminum) frame with rear suspension
Propulsion: Chain drive from pedals with gears

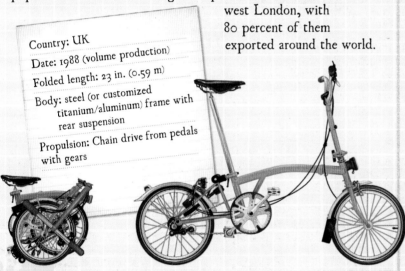

Country: U.S.
Date: 1999
Size: 6 ft (1.8 m) long
Body: lightweight aluminum frame with carbon fiber forks
Propulsion: chain drive from pedals with 18 gears

GTRZ 1000 Racer

Racing bikes have dropped handlebars so the rider can bend down for low wind resistance. They have thin, high-pressured tires and "derailleur" gears using a tight chain that can be moved from one size of sprocket (small, toothed wheel) to another, either at the pedals or at the wheel. Together there can be as many as 21 gears.

Lotus Sport bike

Better known for its sports cars, Lotus came up with a very different looking racing bike in 1992. Chris Boardman of Britain rode one to win a gold medal at the Barcelona Olympics. Instead of traditional steel tubing welded together, this bike was molded using stronger and lighter carbon fiber composite. New "tri-bar" handlebar designs gave the rider an ultra-low position.

Country: UK
Date: 1992
Size: 6 ft (1.8 m) long
Body: lightweight carbon composite frame and wheels
Propulsion: chain drive, no gears

Motorcycles

Motorcycles are two-wheeled vehicles with engines, which a driver straddles as if on a bicycle. Some have a sidecar attached on a third wheel. Mopeds are low-powered motorcycles fitted with pedals to power the engine. Motorcycles also compete in road and cross-country (motocross) racing.

Country: Germany
Date: 1885
Size: 5 ft (1.5 m)
Body: wood and steel
Engine capacity: 264 cc
Speed: under 10 mph (16 km/h)

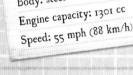

Henderson 7hp

American motorcycles developed as powerful tourers for the big roads in the U.S. This model featured a powerful four-cylinder engine, which was unusual for the time, in a very long frame. The machine was hard to control in tight turns. On the highway, however, it could cruise at over 50 mph (80 km/h).

Country: U.S.
Date: 1913
Size: 5 ¾ ft (1.8 m)
Body: steel
Engine capacity: 1301 cc
Speed: 55 mph (88 km/h)

Daimler Einspur

The Daimler *Einspur* ("single track") may be the first true motorcycle, even though it had extra wheels to keep it stable and a saddle that looked as if it had just been taken off a horse. A tall single-cylinder gasoline engine produced just half a horsepower.

Electra-Glide

Harley-Davidson was founded in 1903. The most famous model the company has ever produced is the 1960s Electra-Glide, which is still in production, little altered from the original. It is popular with many police forces. The heart of the Glide is a big V-twin engine that produces a distinctive "potato-potato" noise.

Country: U.S.
Date: 1965
Size: 6 ½ ft (2 m)
Body: steel
Engine capacity: 1207 cc
Speed: 95 mph (153 km/h)

Vespa GS1 60

The Vespa (Italian for "wasp)" is a scooter — a motorcycle with a little engine mounted around the back wheel so that the rider sits upright with feet together on a platform. It has a "step-through" frame, most controls (except the rear brake) sited on the handlebars, and a powerful enough engine to allow it to zip in and out of traffic. In recent years, the retro design of the Vespa has become very popular again.

Country: Italy
Date: 1963
Size: 5 ½ ft (1.7 m)
Body: steel frame and panels
Engine capacity: 159 cc
Speed: 60 mph (96 km/h)

Honda CB750

With a quiet and revolutionary four-cylinder engine (other bikes had just one or two cylinders), this was the first long-distance touring superbike. When bikes were still thought of as oily and unreliable, the electric-start engine was said to be "sewing-machine-smooth."

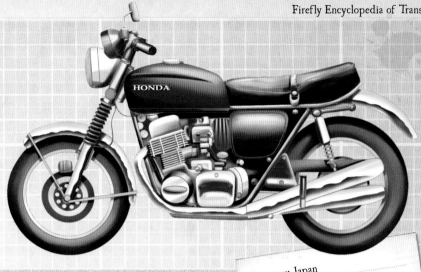

Country: Japan

Date: 1969

Size: 6½ ft (2 m)

Body: steel

Engine capacity: 736 cc

Speed: 120 mph (193 km/h)

Country: Italy

Date: 1972

Size: 7 ft (2.1 m)

Body: steel

Engine capacity: 748 cc

Speed: 126 mph (203 km/h)

Ducati 750SS

Capable of going over 124 mph (200 km/h), this Ducati model was a racing motorcycle for the road. It was also the forerunner of the famous red racers that dominated superbike racing in the 1990s. It had few comforts or frills for the road traveler, and was much more at home screeching at high speed on the racetracks. Its engine was powerful, but the Ducati was also renowned for its fine handling and roadholding.

BMW C1

Perhaps the ultimate commuter vehicle, the BMW C1 runs like a scooter (low-powered engine and low-slung frame with two small wheels). However, a roof, a windshield (and wiper), side protection bars and twin seat belts have been added for extra safety.

Country: Germany

Date: 2000

Size: 6½ ft (2 m)

Body: aluminum frame, plastic body

Engine capacity: 125 cc

Speed: 62 mph (100 km/h)

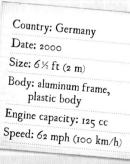

Mobility machines

Transportation has generally been developed on the "one size fits all" principle. It is expensive to adapt a standard mass-produced vehicle that has been designed with the "average" person in mind to suit an individual's convenience and mobility needs. In reality, hardly anyone is average and in recent years there have been a growing number of specialty and customized products that have provided personal mobility to individuals with a disability or where a conventional vehicle cannot easily be used.

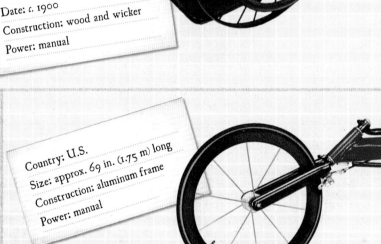

Early wheelchairs

A century ago, wheelchairs like this were expensive handmade products, usually only seen in hospitals, health spas and retirement homes. The chair was heavy and difficult for the seated person to propel by themselves. It was only really suitable for being pushed by someone else over short distances such as along a hospital corridor or seaside promenade. A compact, folding metal wheelchair was not devised until the 1930s.

Date: c. 1900
Construction: wood and wicker
Power: manual

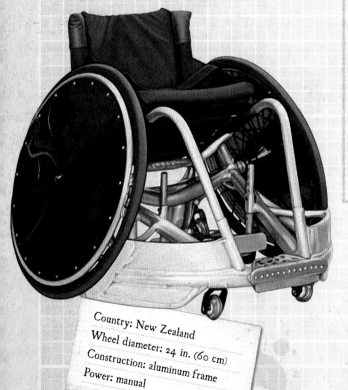

Country: New Zealand
Wheel diameter: 24 in. (60 cm)
Construction: aluminum frame
Power: manual

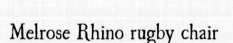

Country: U.S.
Size: approx. 69 in. (1.75 m) long
Construction: aluminum frame
Power: manual

Melrose Rhino rugby chair

Modern self-propelled wheelchairs are designed to be moved by the user pushing on the handrims, which can also be used to steer the chair. Athletes with a disability use specially designed sport wheelchairs that allow them to compete in activities that require speed and agility such as basketball, football and, in this case, rugby. The angled wheels give stability on sharp turns, and the smooth sides provide little grip during tackles.

Country: UK
Date: 2015
Size: 3½ ft (1.07 m) long
Range: up to 16 miles (26 km)
On board: single driver

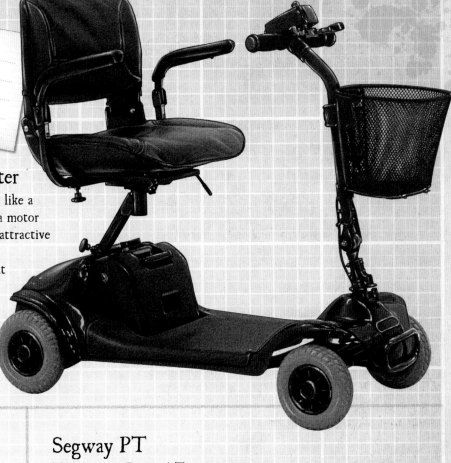

Pro Rider Elite mobility scooter

A mobility scooter offers personal mobility like a powered wheelchair but is configured like a motor scooter. This makes it a cheaper and more attractive option for everyday personal use by many people with mobility problems. It has a seat over three, four or even five wheels, handlebars for steering, and is battery electric powered. A wide range is available, from small, light folding scooters to large, heavy machines suitable for rough outdoor terrain.

Top End Eliminator OSR racing wheelchair

Specialist wheelchairs have been designed for use by people with disabilities in a range of competitive sports. Racing wheelchairs like this one are made from lightweight materials and have an extra front wheel to provide stability at speed. These machines have become more familiar and widely used since the promotion of the International Paralympics alongside the Olympic Games.

Segway PT

The Segway Personal Transporter is a self-balancing battery electric vehicle. The rider stands between the wheels and moves the PT by shifting their weight forward or backward on a platform, turning and steering with the handlebar. Gyroscopic sensors respond to the rider's movements, maintaining balance and speed. The Segway is popular for rental as a novel way to ride around a park or on a guided city tour. It is also used for short distance transportation and patrol by police officers in some countries.

Country: U.S.
Date: 2001
Height: 39 to 49 in. (100 to 125 cm) (adjustable)
Top speed: 12½ mph (20 km/h)
Range: 15 to 24 miles (24 to 39 km)
Construction: steel frame

Emergency vehicles

We often see brightly marked police cars, ambulances, pickup trucks, recovery vans and fire engines with lights flashing or sirens wailing, hurrying through traffic. So it is hard to imagine that the earliest ambulances and fire engines were pulled by horses or people. A modern fire truck can carry 1,000 gallons (4,500 liters) of water through 1,500 ft (450 m) of hose.

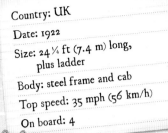

Country: UK
Date: 1922
Size: 24 ¼ ft (7.4 m) long, plus ladder
Body: steel frame and cab
Top speed: 35 mph (56 km/h)
On board: 4

Merryweather fire appliance

This fire engine had one of the early turntable ladders, which could be raised automatically to reach tall buildings quickly. The pump was driven by the truck's engine and could push water through its hoses up to a height of 130 ft (40 m).

Willeme 5471

This aircraft recovery truck was built on a standard Willeme chassis (frame), but was specially adapted to recover aircraft that had broken down. It had 12 wheels on four axles so that it could carry loads of up to 165 tons (150 tonnes). A massive crane on the back was used to lift the aircraft, and the front of the truck had to be very heavy to make sure that it did not tip up.

Country: France
Date: 1956
Size: 35 ft (10.7 m) long
Body: steel frame and cab
Top speed: 37 ½ mph (60 km/h)
On board: 2

FAP riot control

Specially designed to deal with rioting crowds, this van has four-wheel drive for rough or slippery ground and extremely tough bodywork. The exposed glass is armored and the headlights have grills over them. What looks like a gun on the top is a water cannon, powerful enough to knock over and push back rioters. It is supplied from a big tank inside the van.

Fire truck

This truck is very big and it has all kinds of equipment on board. Its ladder has a platform on its top and can go as high as a seven-story building. It can also rotate 360 degrees and the platform has two water cannons that can squirt about 1,222 gallons (5,600 liters) of water a minute onto a fire. Outrigger legs on the side of the truck keep it steady when the platform is being used and the truck has many spotlights and floodlights.

Country: U.S.
Date: 1989
Size: approx. 158 ft (48 m) long
Body: steel and aluminum
Top speed: 105 mph (65 km/h)
On board: 6

Country: Yugoslavia
Date: 1975
Size: 20 ¼ ft (6.2 m) long
Body: armored steel and glass
Top speed: possibly 55 mph (90 km/h)
On board: possibly 2 to 4

Mercedes Sprinter ambulance

Most modern ambulances have customized box bodies built onto a standard van chassis. They have to be tall enough for someone to stand upright in the back, long enough for a stretcher, and have good suspension to give patients and casualties a smooth ride. Most ambulances now have a tail lift for wheelchairs. They all have a loud siren, a range of flashing emergency lights, and a distinctive livery with more high visibility yellow than the traditional ambulance white.

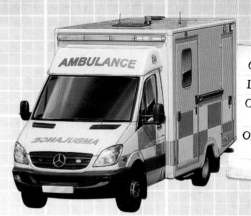

Country: Germany

Date: 2003

Construction: steel chassis and body

On board: 2 crew/paramedics, 2 patients

Eurocopter EC135 air ambulance

Air ambulances can be light aircraft or, more often, helicopters. They were first introduced by the military to evacuate casualties in war zones but now have much wider civilian applications. They are used for the rapid transfer of people who are dangerously ill or seriously injured to a hospital, often landing on a special roof pad. Fitted out with medical equipment, it is the most popular choice for the air ambulance medical services in most European countries. The Eurocopter is also used for police work.

Country: France, Germany

Date: 1996

Size: 33½ ft (10.2 m) long

Cruising speed: 158 mph (254 km/h)

On board: 1 pilot, 2 paramedics, 2 patients

Wrecker

This piece of equipment took well over a year to complete and is designed for towing and heavy duty recovery. The truck was made separately from the wrecker body. The wrecker body was built in Texas and mounted onto the stretched-out frame of the truck which came from another part of the U.S.

Country: U.S.

Date: 1997

Size: 39 ft (12 m) long

Body: steel

Top speed: approx. 56 mph (90 km/h)

On board: 1, sometimes 2

Severn class lifeboat

Lifeboats attend vessels in distress inshore or out at sea in order to rescue the crew and passengers. The Severn class is the UK's largest and best-equipped lifeboat type, designed for use in all weather conditions. Each boat is self-righting and if knocked over at sea in the most extreme weather will automatically right itself within a few seconds. All UK lifeboats are run by the Royal National Lifeboat Institution (RNLI) and crewed entirely by volunteers.

Country: UK

Date: 1992

Size: 57 ft (17.3 m) long

Construction: steel, fiberglass

On board: 7 crew

Who invented the wheel?

The first wheels were made in about 3500 BC in Mesopotamia, the area between the Tigris and Euphrates rivers, in what is now Iraq. No one knows the names of the craftsmen who made these early wheels, but they probably got the idea from potters, who were using spinning wheels to make vessels out of clay. Like the potters' wheels, these early cartwheels were made out of solid wood. Some 2,000 years later, fast two-wheeled chariots ran on spoked wheels. After another 2,000 years, there were metal wheels, improved wheel bearings, and air-filled tires for a bump-free ride.

Primitive wheels were made of planks of wood held together with wooden pegs and mounted on axles. These **solid wheels** were used on carts to carry peat and on primitive chariots, and were very heavy to pull. Craftsmen from Mesopotamia (now in modern Iraq) removed some of the wood to make a wheel with two large holes, the forerunner of the spoked wheel.

Tires were first fitted to wheels by the ancient Egyptians, who covered the rims of their wooden wheels with leather to protect them from wear. Solid rubber tires appeared in the 1840s, and in 1888 John Boyd Dunlop fitted his son's bicycle (shown here) with **inflatable rubber tires**. Today, most road vehicles have inflatable tires.

Today, tires can be manufactured in gigantic proportions. The largest are used in the construction and mining industries, where vehicles need to shift heavy loads over rough terrain, and can be as much as 14 ft (4 m) tall.

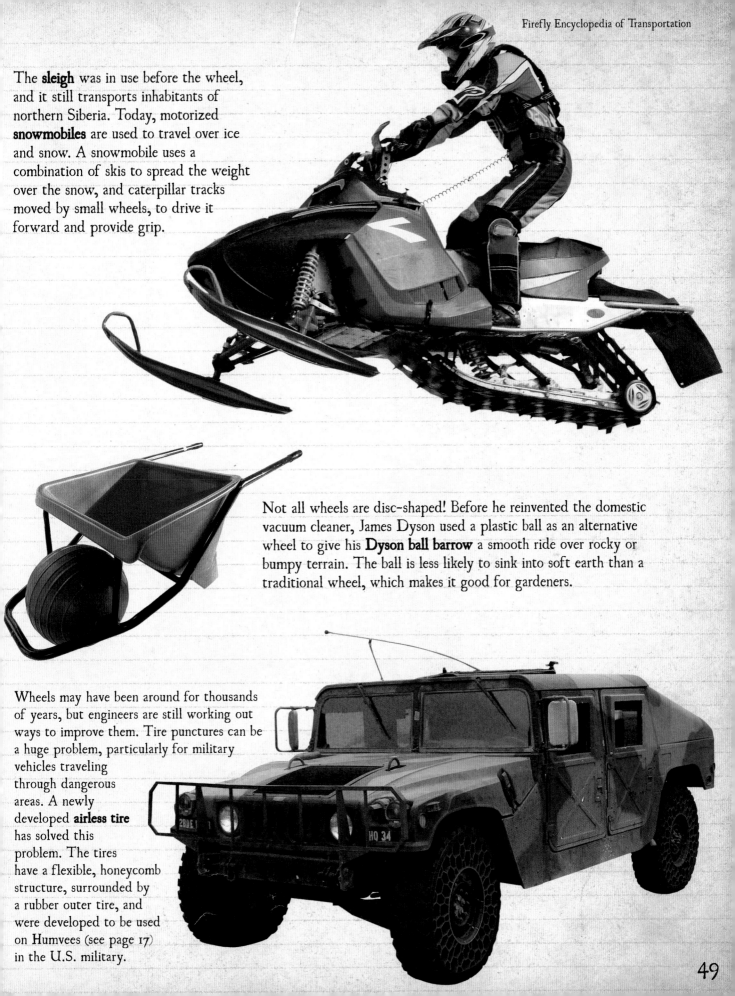

The **sleigh** was in use before the wheel, and it still transports inhabitants of northern Siberia. Today, motorized **snowmobiles** are used to travel over ice and snow. A snowmobile uses a combination of skis to spread the weight over the snow, and caterpillar tracks moved by small wheels, to drive it forward and provide grip.

Not all wheels are disc-shaped! Before he reinvented the domestic vacuum cleaner, James Dyson used a plastic ball as an alternative wheel to give his **Dyson ball barrow** a smooth ride over rocky or bumpy terrain. The ball is less likely to sink into soft earth than a traditional wheel, which makes it good for gardeners.

Wheels may have been around for thousands of years, but engineers are still working out ways to improve them. Tire punctures can be a huge problem, particularly for military vehicles traveling through dangerous areas. A newly developed **airless tire** has solved this problem. The tires have a flexible, honeycomb structure, surrounded by a rubber outer tire, and were developed to be used on Humvees (see page 17) in the U.S. military.

49

ON WATER

Boats and ships are the most varied of all forms of transportation, ranging from tiny dinghies about six feet long to vast supertankers that take more than five minutes to walk along. From warships to windsurfers, there are vessels for virtually any task.

In the Stone Age, the earliest boat was a canoe hollowed out of a log. Then came oars and sails followed by steam and gasoline engines. Today, wave-piercing water jets and solar power can propel ships — and the water speed record is now a staggering 317 mph (511 km/h).

Cruise ship in Geiranger Fjord, Norway (below)

Luxury liners take vacationing passengers to exotic ports around the world. Such vessels have never been more popular. The biggest cruise ships reach over 1,150 ft (350 m) in length and can carry up to 6,300 passengers.

Dragonfly yacht

| Square sail | Lateen sail | Settee sail | Gaff sail | Lug sail | Sprit sail |

What is a ship?

Any large vessel that floats on the water can be called a ship. Smaller craft are called boats, and sailors often say that if a vessel is big enough to carry a boat, then that vessel is a ship. Every ship has a body called a hull, which in ancient times was made of wood but is now more likely to be metal. Ships also have some means of propulsion, such as sails or an engine. They have been around for well over 10,000 years, and are used as warships or pleasure craft, and to carry cargo or passengers.

Types of sail

There are dozens of types of sail. Western oceangoing ships most commonly used square sails which, in a fully rigged ship, could set three or more to a mast. Triangular sails, such as lateen sails or settees, are still favored in the Arab world.

Parts of a sailing ship

There are several vertical masts, with other timbers, such as horizontal yards, to support the sails. The bow (front) is often pointed, to cut smoothly through the water; the rudder, which is used for steering, is at the stern (rear).

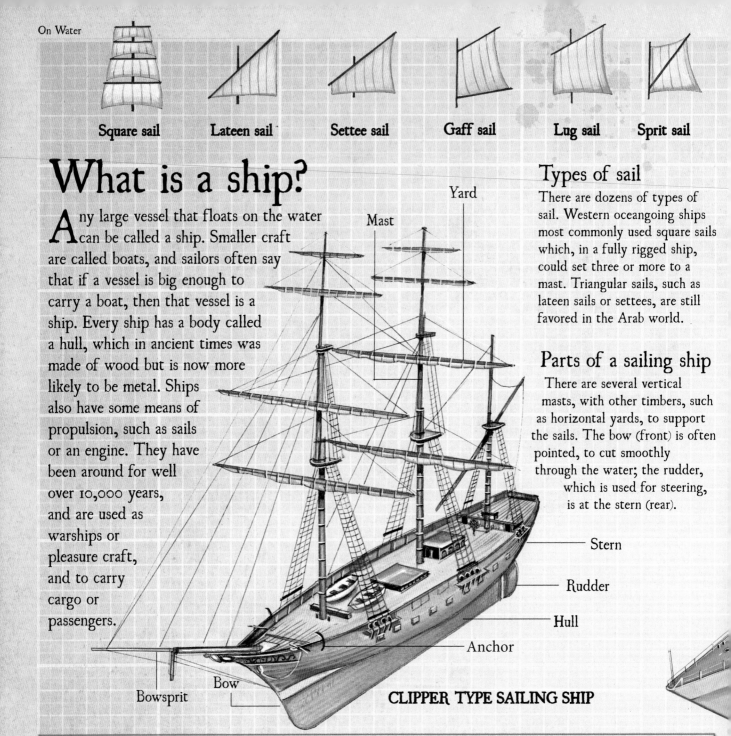

Mast

Yard

Stern

Rudder

Hull

Anchor

Bowsprit

Bow

CLIPPER TYPE SAILING SHIP

How a ship floats

A solid object sinks because it weighs more than the amount of water it displaces. All ships are hollow and therefore very light for their size. They only settle into the water until the amount that they displace equals their own total weight. The pressure of the water from below then supports the rest of the ship above the surface.

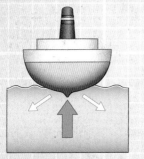

The weight of the boat displaces the water.

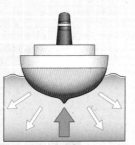

The displaced water now equals the weight of the boat and the boat floats.

Hovercraft

Instead of floating, a hovercraft hovers on a cushion of air just above the surface of the water or a swamp (or dry land). It has huge fans to create the air cushion, which is held in place by a rubber membrane, called a skirt. This stretches all around the hull.

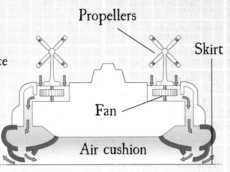

Propellers

Skirt

Fan

Air cushion

Propulsion

Ships used to have sails or oars, but modern ships usually have an engine. This drives a number of propellers, which push the craft through the water. The first propellers had twin blades, but three- or four-bladed propellers are more efficient and powerful.

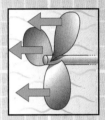

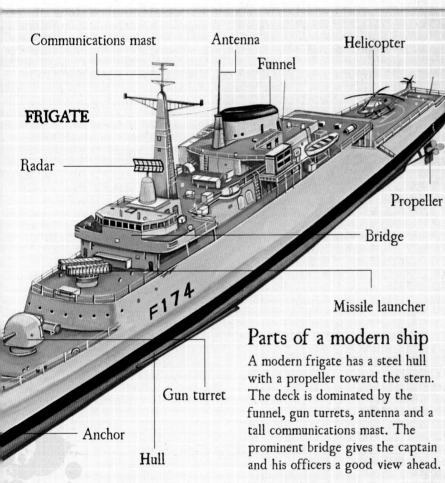

FRIGATE

Communications mast

Antenna

Funnel

Helicopter

Radar

Propeller

Bridge

F174

Missile launcher

Gun turret

Anchor

Hull

Parts of a modern ship

A modern frigate has a steel hull with a propeller toward the stern. The deck is dominated by the funnel, gun turrets, antenna and a tall communications mast. The prominent bridge gives the captain and his officers a good view ahead.

Diving a submarine

A submarine contains large ballast (weight) tanks (heavily weighted with water): these can be filled or emptied as the vessel moves. When the captain wants to dive, he orders the tanks to be filled with water. This increases the weight and density of the submarine, which makes the vessel sink. To rise back to the surface, the water is pumped out from the tanks.

Surfacing

Diving

Ballast tanks empty

Ballast tanks being emptied

Ballast tanks filling

Hydrofoils

One thing that slows ships down is the force, called drag, created by the hull in the water. Hydrofoils get around this problem by raising their hull out of the water on special struts, called foils. Hydrofoils sit in the water like normal craft, but as they gather speed, the foils come into play, lifting up the hulls. This means that these craft can go much faster than standard vessels of the same power.

Hydrofoil in water

Hydrofoil out of water

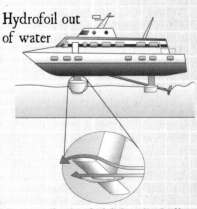

At speed, the foil lifts the hull out of the water.

Venturing onto water

Many of the first boats, including the North American kayak and the Polynesian outrigger, were so well crafted that similar boats are still used to transport people and goods 5,000 years later. When people first began to build boats, some chopped down tree trunks to make rafts or canoes, while others chose thin branches and animal skins to make frame boats. Ancient sailing vessels such as dhows and junks are still made today and sail in the Arabian and China seas.

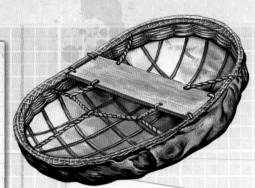

Country: Ireland, Wales
Date: from pre-history
Size: 6½ ft (2 m) long
Construction: hide on wicker framework
Speed: about 3½ mph (6 km/h)
On board: 1

Dugout canoe

The canoe was probably the first type of boat to be made. It consists of a tree trunk shaped and hollowed out in the middle to make a place where people could sit and paddle. Early people used simple stone axes to carve the wood to get the best hull shape. They used fire to hollow out the middle.

Country: worldwide
Date: from pre-history
Size: 10 ft (3 m) long
Construction: wood
Speed: about 3½ to 7 mph (6 to 11 km/h)
On board: 2

Coracle

Shaped so that it can be carried on the back, the coracle is an early lightweight boat. The design drawback is that it is not very stable in the water. The user needs to be experienced to keep it under control with only a simple wooden spade-like paddle. Like the kayak and similar portable boats, it is still used, mainly for fishing.

Country: Canada
Date: from pre-history
Size: 18 ft (5.5 m) long
Construction: seal skin on wood or bone frame
Speed: about 3½ to 7 mph (6 to 11 km/h)
On board: 1

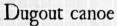

Wooden raft

The most basic water craft of all is the wooden raft. It is pushed along with a pole, and is made of several logs lashed together with vines, twine or some other binding material. Early raft-builders realized quite quickly that their craft worked better if the logs had pointed ends, or if the entire raft front had a pointed shape.

Inuit kayak

For thousands of years, the Inuit people of Canada and Russia, and the Eskimo people of Alaska have built kayaks — long, narrow boats made of a wood or whalebone framework covered with skins. Kayaks are used for hunting and fishing, and their light weight makes them easy to carry. Their design makes them easy to return quickly to their upright position if they capsize.

Country: worldwide
Date: from pre-history
Size: 6½ ft (2 m) long
Construction: wood
Speed: about 3½ to 7 mph (6 to 11 km/h)
On board: 1 or more

Pacific outrigger

This type of boat was built by the sailors of the Pacific islands. The outriggers gave the craft great stability on the Pacific surf, in spite of the narrow hull. This type of hull with its large sail could travel very fast, and early navigators covered thousands of miles in boats like these.

Arab dhow

With their sleek wooden hulls, flat sterns and lateen (triangular) sails, the dhows of the Arab world are easy to recognize. They have one or two masts, and the lateen rig is especially good for sailing with winds from the side. They are used in the Red Sea, Indian Ocean and Persian Gulf. Some dhows now have diesel engines.

Chinese junk

The junk is the traditional Chinese sailing ship that evolved in medieval times. The hull is made differently from that of a Western ship. Instead of getting its strength from a keel, the hull is divided by bulkheads (wooden partitions) that make the structure rigid. The sails are made of narrow strips of cloth held on bamboo battens.

Oars and sails

All early civilizations depended on sea and river transportation. The ancient Egyptians traveled up and down the Nile River. The Greeks and Romans sailed all around the Mediterranean, relying on ships for both trade and war. These civilizations built the first sailing ships and developed the use of rows of oarsmen, who could propel a ship steadily and at speed over short distances. In addition, the Romans improved the steering oar, making their ships easier to move in battle.

Country: Egypt
Date: c. 2000 BC
Size: 39 ft (12 m) long
Construction: cedar wood
Sail material: flax (linen)
On board: 10

Egyptian wooden boat

Among the world's first sailing vessels was this Egyptian wooden-hulled, single-masted and square-sail boat. The rich used them to travel along the Nile. A steersman controlled the boat with a large oar at the rear, and there were also long poles that the crew could use to push the vessel off sand banks. Larger versions were used to carry cattle and other cargo.

Country: Greece
Date: c. 480 BC
Size: 148 ft (45 m) long
Construction: wood
Sail material: flax (linen)
On board: 190

Greek trireme

Sleek, fast and deadly, the Greek trireme was one of the most powerful warships of the ancient world. The term "trireme" means "three oars," and this type of ship had three tiers of oars — upper, middle and lower — on each side of the hull. Each oar was over 14 ft (4 m) long. Together with a square sail, this gave the trireme an impressive turn of speed — either to get out of trouble or to batter an enemy vessel with its fearsome ram.

Egyptian reed boat

Bundles of reeds were tied together with twine to make this early fishing boat. The papyrus reed — also used to make a paperlike writing material — was ideal for the job. It was light, easy to work and grew plentifully by the banks of the Nile.

Country: Egypt
Date: c. 3000 BC
Size: 20 ft (6 m) long
Construction: papyrus reeds
Sail material: flax (linen)
On board: 4 or 5

Phoenician trader

The sea-trading Phoenicians built broad and deep-framed ships to carry cargoes of cloth and glassware around the Mediterranean. Their ships could have sails, oars or both. These sturdy timber vessels voyaged as far as Cornwall and Ireland.

Country: Mediterranean area
Date: c. 1200 BC
Size: from 82 ft (25 m) long
Construction: wood
Sail material: flax (linen)
On board: 30

Roman merchantman

The Romans needed large ships to carry goods around their huge empire. Their merchant ships were solidly built and broad. With one mast, usually rigged with a single, square sail, they were not very fast. However, they could carry up to 275 tons (250 tonnes) of cargo. There was extra space and height on the "poop deck" (aft).

Country: Mediterranean area

Date: 1st century BC

Size: 148 ft (45 m) long

Construction: wood

Sail material: flax (linen)

On board: 120

Country: Mediterranean area

Date: 1st century BC

Size: 98 ft (30 m) long

Construction: wood

Sail material: flax (linen)

On board: 30

Roman galley

Roman warships were called galleys, and they could have two or three tiers of oars. The oarsmen were usually slaves or criminals. The Roman navy also used sails for extra speed, and they attacked their enemies by ramming. Galleys would also come alongside and throw out a wooden bridge for soldiers to swarm on to enemy ships.

Viking longship

These elegant ships with their decorated prows were feared for bringing Vikings on raids along the coasts of Europe. All had a single mast, a square sail and up to 34 ports for oars on each side. Smaller versions were used along rivers and broader ones for cargo.

Country: Northern Europe area

Date: c. 850 AD

Size: from 69 ft (21 m) long

Construction: wood

Sail material: wool

On board: 34

57

Sailing to new worlds

Sailing the uncharted oceans in the 1400s was like traveling to the planets today. Carracks, caravels and similar sailing ships took European navigators to new worlds. Early sailing ships were small with square sails and lateen (triangular) sails, and sometimes both. The three-masted, square-rigged ship remained little changed for several hundred years.

Country: Northern Europe
Date: 13th to 15th centuries
Size: 82 ft (25 m) long
Construction: wood
Sail material: flax or hemp
On board: 12

Caravel

This type of ship was favored by many of the great Portuguese and Spanish explorers, including Christopher Columbus. The caravel was quite narrow and light in weight. It had a square stern and a curved prow. A caravel usually had three masts and these were rigged with triangular sails, which could take advantage of side winds. Some caravels also carried a square sail.

Country: Southern Europe
Date: 15th and 16th centuries
Size: 98 ft (30 m) long
Construction: wood
Sail material: flax or hemp
On board: 25 to 40

Cog

A sturdy cargo vessel, the cog was steered with a rudder, which hung from a straight stern post. There were small raised decks, called the forecastle and aftercastle, at either end of the ship. The sail was square.

Carrack

These could be ships of over 1,100 tons (1,000 tonnes), carrying a large load of cargo because their hulls were deep and high-sided. They were also very strong, with as many as four long reinforcing timbers, called wales, running along the length of the hull. Carracks usually had three masts (sometimes four), the main mast being much taller than the others. They were also used as warships.

Country: Portugal, Spain
Date: 15th and 16th centuries
Size: 131 ft (40 m) long
Construction: wood
Sail material: flax or hemp
On board: 40

Galleon

Galleons were tall fighting ships with elegant, pointed prows and high aftercastles that could be decorated with rich carving and gilding. They carried rows of cannons, which fired through square gun ports on the sides of the ship. The extra weight of these heavy guns could have made the galleon unstable, but the ship's inward-sloping sides helped keep it steady.

Country: Europe

Date: 17th century

Size: 125 ft (38 m) long

Construction: wood

Sail material: flax or hemp

On board: 142

Country: Southern Europe

Date: 15th and 16th centuries

Size: 131 ft (40 m) long

Construction: wood, clinker built

Sail material: flax or hemp

On board: 40 or more

Mayflower

The *Mayflower* was similar to a small galleon, but with only a handful of guns. The decks were used for cramming in supplies and passengers who were the early settlers of North America, known as the Pilgrims. The crew had a cabin and galley in the forecastle.

Pinnace

Smaller than a galleon, a pinnace could be either rowed or sailed. It was a three-masted vessel with a large aftercastle and a tapering prow. The ship was square-rigged, but the rear mast could be rigged with just a triangular sail.

Country: Northern Europe

Date: 17th and 18th centuries

Size: 148 ft (45 m) long

Construction: wood

Sail material: flax or hemp

On board: 45 or more

Dutch East Indiaman

The islands of Indonesia were known as the Spice Islands or the East Indies. Many European merchants traded there and in China and India. They used East Indiamen to bring back their cargoes. The ships had large hulls with plenty of cargo space. They had three masts and also carried many guns on their upper decks to protect themselves against attack.

Country: Northern Europe

Date: 13th to 15th centuries

Size: 82 ft (25 m) long

Construction: wood

Sail material: flax or hemp

On board: 12

Big sailing ships

From the 17th century, seafaring nations such as Britain and Holland began to acquire large worldwide empires. They needed larger ships to carry all sorts of cargoes — spices, tea, slaves and sugar — to and from their colonies across the oceans. These bigger ships also carried more sails, making them faster and more maneuverable. Some of these vessels, such as the clippers, could sail from London to Shanghai in under 100 days.

Country: Europe
Date: 18th to 19th centuries
Size: 394 ft (120 m) long
Construction: wood
Sail fabric: flax or hemp
On board: 800

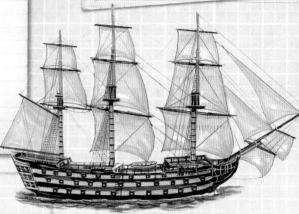

Country: Europe
Date: 18th century
Size: 131 ft (40 m) long
Construction: wood
Sail fabric: flax or hemp
On board: 90

Endeavour

British Captain James Cook set off in 1768 for his explorations to the Pacific in a ship originally designed to carry coal in the rough North Sea. The solidly built *Endeavour* had plenty of room in the hold for supplies, plant specimens, carvings and other items Cook collected.

Man-of-war

These warships usually had one to three decks of cannons. A three-decker could carry over 100 guns. They were designed to get the captain within range of the enemy so that a "broadside" of cannonballs could be fired.

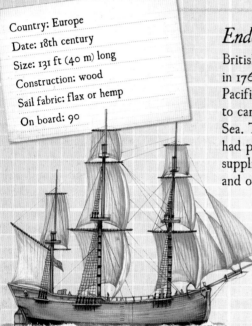

Country: U.S.
Date: 19th century
Size: 180 ft (55 m) long
Construction: wood
Sail fabric: cotton or hemp
On board: 28

Thomas W. Lawson

A schooner is a sailing ship with two or more masts and the lower sails rigged along the length of the vessel. Most were coastal or medium-range cargo vessels but some were huge ocean-going schooners. The *Thomas W. Lawson* is the biggest ever built. She had seven masts but used engines to help a very small crew hoist her sails.

Country: U.S.
Date: 1902
Size: 395 ft (120 m) long
Construction: wood planking on iron
Sail fabric: flax or hemp
On board: about 20

Frigate

Frigates carry their main weapons on a single deck. The U.S. Navy designed large and speedy frigates to defend shipping from attacks by pirates — especially Barbary corsairs from North Africa. Some American frigates had 44 guns.

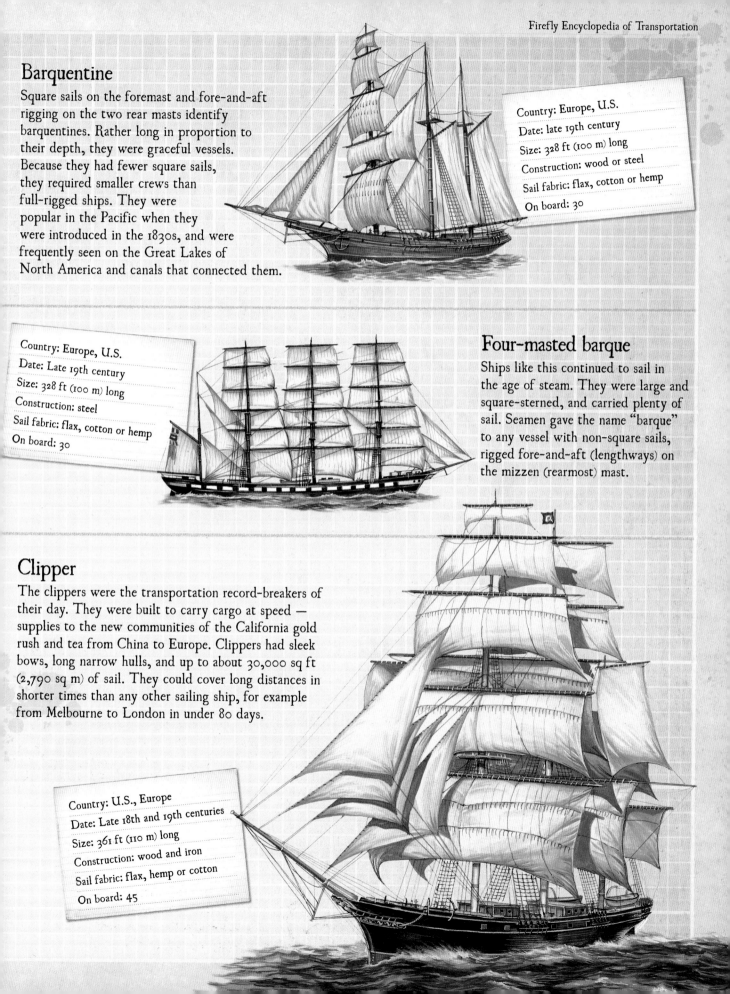

Barquentine

Square sails on the foremast and fore-and-aft rigging on the two rear masts identify barquentines. Rather long in proportion to their depth, they were graceful vessels. Because they had fewer square sails, they required smaller crews than full-rigged ships. They were popular in the Pacific when they were introduced in the 1830s, and were frequently seen on the Great Lakes of North America and canals that connected them.

Country: Europe, U.S.
Date: late 19th century
Size: 328 ft (100 m) long
Construction: wood or steel
Sail fabric: flax, cotton or hemp
On board: 30

Country: Europe, U.S.
Date: Late 19th century
Size: 328 ft (100 m) long
Construction: steel
Sail fabric: flax, cotton or hemp
On board: 30

Four-masted barque

Ships like this continued to sail in the age of steam. They were large and square-sterned, and carried plenty of sail. Seamen gave the name "barque" to any vessel with non-square sails, rigged fore-and-aft (lengthways) on the mizzen (rearmost) mast.

Clipper

The clippers were the transportation record-breakers of their day. They were built to carry cargo at speed — supplies to the new communities of the California gold rush and tea from China to Europe. Clippers had sleek bows, long narrow hulls, and up to about 30,000 sq ft (2,790 sq m) of sail. They could cover long distances in shorter times than any other sailing ship, for example from Melbourne to London in under 80 days.

Country: U.S., Europe
Date: Late 18th and 19th centuries
Size: 361 ft (110 m) long
Construction: wood and iron
Sail fabric: flax, hemp or cotton
On board: 45

Full steam ahead

For thousands of years, ships could only steer a course that the wind or oar power allowed. Then, in the 19th century, the steam engine brought about a mechanical revolution in sea transportation. Steamships could steer almost any course at any time, and at a regular speed. The first steamship, *Pyroscaphe*, was built in France in 1783. Early steamships had paddle wheels. Propellers took over in the 1840s. Sails continued to be carried until the 1860s, when marine engines had become more reliable.

Charlotte Dundas

The first practical steamship, the *Charlotte Dundas*, towed barges on the River Clyde in Scotland for three or four weeks in 1802. It was powered by a single-cylinder 12 horsepower engine driving a paddle wheel. The vessel was taken out of service because of damage to the river banks caused by the wash from its paddle wheel.

Country: UK
Date: 1837
Size: 236 ft (72 m) long
Construction: wood, iron
  reinforcements
Top speed: 10 mph (15.75 km/h)
On board: 148

Country: UK
Date: 1801
Size: 58 ft (17.7 m) long
Construction: wood
Top speed: 4 mph (6.5 km/h)
On board: 6

Great Western

The *Great Western* was designed by Isambard Kingdom Brunel in 1837 and built of oak. It had four steam engines driving both paddle wheels and a propeller and was the first ship to have enough coal for a nonstop voyage. It set out on its first transatlantic voyage on April 8, 1838 and docked in New York 15 days and 5 hours later.

Savannah

The *Savannah* was the first steamship to cross the Atlantic Ocean. It was a sailing vessel fitted with steam engines and paddle wheels. It made its historic voyage from Savannah, Georgia to Liverpool, England in 27 days. Its wood-burning engines were used to drive two paddle wheels for only a small part of the crossing but enough to prove that steamships were practical oceangoing vessels.

Country: U.S.
Date: 1819
Size: 98½ ft (30 m) long
Construction: wood
Top speed: 9 mph (15 km/h)
On board: 42

Country: UK
Date: 1838
Size: 692 ft (211 m) long
Construction: wood
Top speed: 15 mph (24 km/h)
On board: 3,500

Britannia

Britannia was a wooden paddle steamer and the first transatlantic passenger liner. Its ocean service began in 1840. As part of a fleet of passenger steamers, it offered a twice-monthly passage all year round between Liverpool and Boston.

Country: UK
Date: 1840
Size: 212 ft (64.7 m) long
Construction: wood
Top speed: 10 mph (15.75 km/h)
On board: 204

Country: UK
Date: 1856
Size: 377 ft (115 m) long
Construction: iron
Top speed: 15 ½ mph (25 km/h)
On board: 250

Persia

The *Persia* was the world's largest liner until the *Great Eastern* was built. It was also one of the last to be powered by paddles — they were huge at 40 ft (12 m) across — rather than by a screw propeller.

Great Britain

Brunel's second transatlantic ship was also the first iron-hulled steamship. He designed it with paddle wheels but these were changed for a propeller. In 1970, its rusting hull was brought to Bristol docks, where it was originally built, and restored.

Country: UK
Date: 1843
Size: 322 ft (98 m) long
Construction: iron
Top speed: 13 mph (20 km/h)
On board: 260

Great Eastern

When the *Great Eastern* was built, it was five times the size of any other ship. It was powered by a screw propeller and paddle wheels, and carried enough coal to reach Australia without refueling. It failed as a liner but successfully laid the first transatlantic telegraph cable in 1866 on its second attempt.

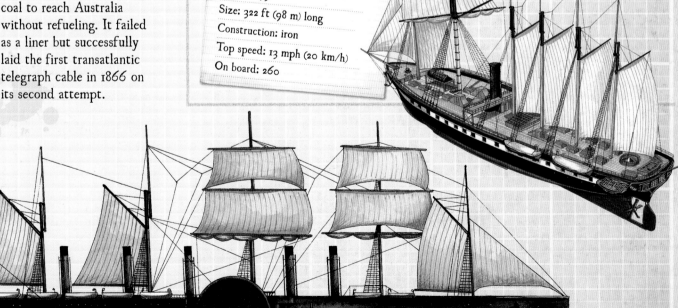

Luxury liners

Steamships began carrying passengers and mail across the Atlantic in 1838. By the 1890s, liners were designed to accommodate hundreds of passengers in the sort of luxury usually found in the best hotels. Swimming pools, dance floors, opulent lounges and restaurants catered to the wealthy first-class travelers. Below water, a row of watertight bulkheads (walls) stretched across each vessel, dividing it into separate compartments to keep it afloat if one part of the hull was damaged. Modern cruise ships carry 4.5 million people every year.

Turbinia

This was the first vessel to be driven by a steam turbine. In this type of engine, high-pressure steam pushes on a series of blades that are fixed to a metal shaft. When the blades move, the shaft turns, making the ship's propeller spin around.

Country: UK
Date: 1894
Size: 105 ft (32 m) long
Construction: steel
Top speed: 32¾ mph (61 km/h)
On board: 5

King Edward

The first merchant ship to be powered by the kind of turbines used in the *Turbinia* was the *King Edward*. The vessel's powerful engines propelled the ship on passenger services up and down the River Clyde and on cruises along the Scottish coast. The ship was used to carry troops during World War II before being broken up in 1952.

Country: UK
Date: 1901
Size: 328 ft (100 m) long
Construction: steel
Top speed: 23½ mph (38 km/h)
On board: 200

Titanic

With interiors based on a French royal palace, the *Titanic* was very luxurious. It was the largest ship of its time. But on April 12, 1912, its maiden voyage, it hit an iceberg and sank in the Atlantic Ocean, off the coast of Newfoundland. There were too few lifeboats and 1,500 people drowned. Now all ships have to carry enough lifeboats and life jackets for all those on board.

Country: UK
Date: 1912
Size: 853 ft (260 m) long
Construction: steel
Top speed: 22 mph (41 km/h)
On board: 3,511

Bremen

The German-built *Bremen* was designed to be the fastest transatlantic liner. The record had been set 20 years before by Britain's *Mauretania* at 26 mph (48 km/h). *Bremen* beat the record. It was also more spacious than its rival, with an extra 131 ft (40 m) of hull space for the same number of passengers and crew.

Country: Germany
Date: 1929
Size: 938 ft (286 m) long
Construction: steel
Top speed: 28 mph (52 km/h)
On board: 2,990

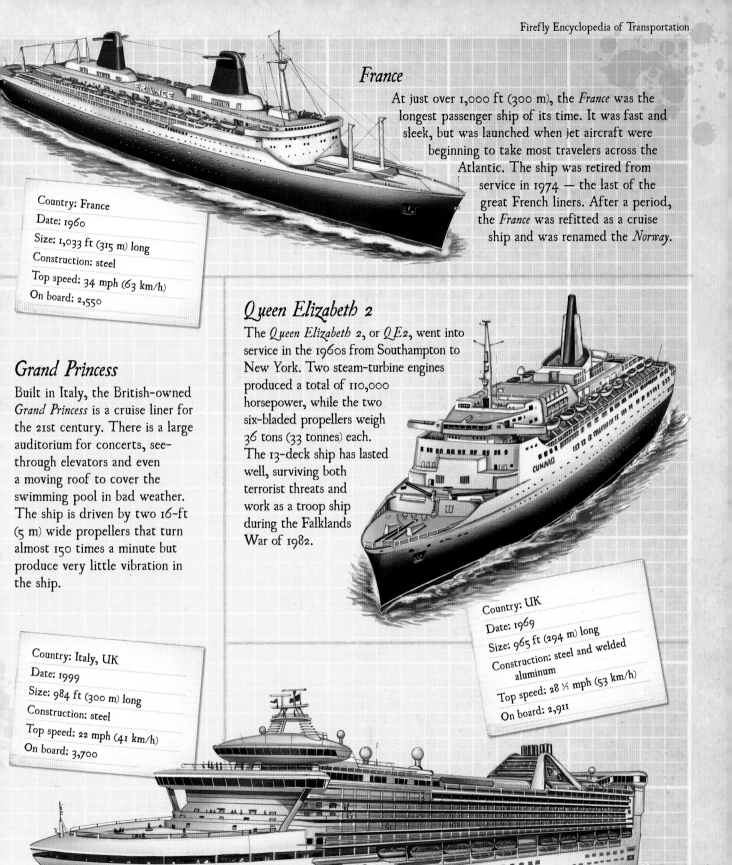

France

At just over 1,000 ft (300 m), the *France* was the longest passenger ship of its time. It was fast and sleek, but was launched when jet aircraft were beginning to take most travelers across the Atlantic. The ship was retired from service in 1974 — the last of the great French liners. After a period, the *France* was refitted as a cruise ship and was renamed the *Norway*.

Country: France
Date: 1960
Size: 1,033 ft (315 m) long
Construction: steel
Top speed: 34 mph (63 km/h)
On board: 2,550

Grand Princess

Built in Italy, the British-owned *Grand Princess* is a cruise liner for the 21st century. There is a large auditorium for concerts, see-through elevators and even a moving roof to cover the swimming pool in bad weather. The ship is driven by two 16-ft (5 m) wide propellers that turn almost 150 times a minute but produce very little vibration in the ship.

Queen Elizabeth 2

The *Queen Elizabeth 2*, or *QE2*, went into service in the 1960s from Southampton to New York. Two steam-turbine engines produced a total of 110,000 horsepower, while the two six-bladed propellers weigh 36 tons (33 tonnes) each. The 13-deck ship has lasted well, surviving both terrorist threats and work as a troop ship during the Falklands War of 1982.

Country: UK
Date: 1969
Size: 965 ft (294 m) long
Construction: steel and welded aluminum
Top speed: 28 ½ mph (53 km/h)
On board: 2,911

Country: Italy, UK
Date: 1999
Size: 984 ft (300 m) long
Construction: steel
Top speed: 22 mph (41 km/h)
On board: 3,700

Fighting ships

With the coming of steam power, the way the warships looked and operated changed. Sails and wooden hulls were replaced with screw propellers and iron hulls. Warships became faster, easier to maneuver and had more space for newer and bigger guns that fired explosive shells. Modern navies use a variety of different craft, from huge aircraft carriers to nuclear-powered submarines and smaller multi-task ships.

Warrior

Driven by both steam and sail, the *Warrior* was the first oceangoing iron-clad battleship in the world. Thick armored plates were bolted to a teak hull to give massive protection. The ship also carried 36 powerful guns, making it the most heavily armed ship at the time.

Country: UK
Date: 1859
Size: 420 ft (116 m) long
Construction: wood, iron armor
Top speed: 17 mph (31.5 km/h)
On board: 707

Merrimack vs *Monitor*

The U.S. Civil War between the Northern and Southern states (1861–65) saw the first battle between metal-armored, steam-driven ships. The North's all-iron battleship *Monitor* lay low in the water, bearing a single turret with two guns. The South's *Merrimack* was fitted with sloping iron armor over its deck.

Country: U.S.
Date: 1862
Size: *Monitor* 172 ft (52 m) long; *Merrimack* 263 ft (80 m) long
Construction: wood, iron armor
Top speed: *Monitor* 6 mph (11 km/h); *Merrimack* 9 mph (17 km/h)
On board: *Monitor* 49; *Merrimack* 330

Dreadnought

The steel-plated *Dreadnought* was the first modern battleship. It had heavy guns mounted on five turrets that could be fired at the same time. A telephone linked each turret to a control platform.

Country: UK
Date: 1906
Size: 526 ft (160 m) long
Construction: steel
Top speed: 21 mph (39 km/h)
On board: 773

Lightning

Torpedo missiles that travel underwater to their target were developed in the 1860s and 1870s. Navies quickly set about building ships to fire torpedoes. The *Lightning* was one of the first British torpedo boats and was also used to defend coastal bases from enemy attack.

Country: UK
Date: 1877
Size: 84 ft (26 m) long
Construction: wood
Top speed: 20 mph (33 km/h)
On board: 35

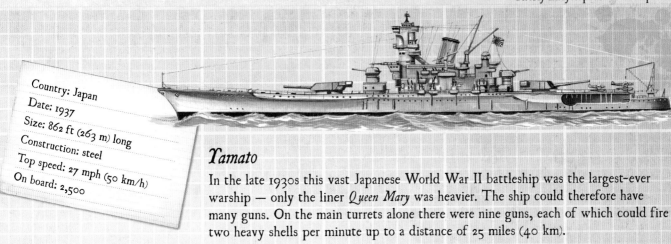

Yamato

In the late 1930s this vast Japanese World War II battleship was the largest-ever warship — only the liner *Queen Mary* was heavier. The ship could therefore have many guns. On the main turrets alone there were nine guns, each of which could fire two heavy shells per minute up to a distance of 25 miles (40 km).

MEKO-class frigate

Escort vessels, such as the MEKO series, are used to protect aircraft carriers, groups of submarines or convoys of ships. The name is an abbreviation for a German word meaning "multi-purpose." The basic hull is designed so that different weapons and equipment can be fitted when needed.

USS *Virginia*

The warship USS *Virginia* was powered by a nuclear reactor. The reactor heats water to produce steam, which drives a turbine as in a regular steamship. The advantage of nuclear power is that the vessel can sail vast distances without having to stop for fuel: one fueling alone can take such a ship three times around the world. However, there is a big safety risk, in spite of the fact that onboard reactors have protective shields weighing as much as 1,100 tons (1,000 tonnes). In addition, only a few specialized depots can make repairs to this type of ship.

Powerboats

Powered craft can be anything from a small dinghy with an outboard motor to a high-speed racing vessel. But for most people, a "powerboat" means a racing craft built for speeds of up to 57 mph (90 km/h) or more. There are many types, but most are made with planing hulls — in other words, they are designed to rise up out of the water as they pick up speed, to reduce drag and help them go even faster. They are often built with modern materials, such as layers of fiberglass sandwiched with lightweight balsa wood. This cuts down weight and improves performance still further.

Water-jet engine

A water-jet engine takes in water through a duct and forces it out at speed and at high pressure, through the stern of the unit. The result is that the boat is pushed forward in the opposite direction to the jet of water.

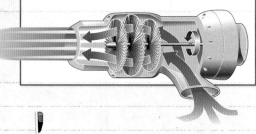

Around-the-world powered record

The slender hull of the *Cable & Wireless Adventurer* is designed to slice through the waves at up to 28 mph (45 km/h). Its twin turbo-diesel engines are powerful and efficient, cutting down the need for refueling. With 16 crew members, the 115-ft (35-m), 57-ton (52-tonne) powerboat set off in April 1998 to break the around-the-world record for a motor-powered vessel. It took 75 days and the craft had cut 9 days off the previous record.

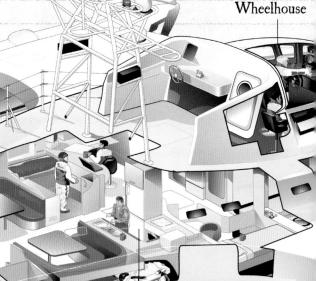

Antenna

Global Positioning System antenna

Radar

Wheelhouse

Rubber dinghy

Galley

8.3-liter turbo-diesel engine

CABLE & WIRELESS ADVENTURER

Hydroplane racer **Pleasure craft** **Offshore racer** **Formula One racer**

Powerboat types

Powerboats can be pleasure craft designed to carry one or more people and to give them a taste of speed. Offshore racers go faster, and even monohull designs lift out of the water as they reach top speed. Hydroplanes race at speeds of over 100 mph (160 km/h) while the powerful **Formula One craft** (right) have 300 horsepower engines capable of 125 mph (200 km/h) and sharp right-angled turns.

Crew quarters

Wave-piercing hull

Fiberglass body

Stabilizer

VSVs

The Very Slender Vessel (VSV) is a powerboat with a long, thin hull with deep and narrow sides. These give both stability and sharp turning in the water. The VSV tends to push or pierce its way in and under the waves rather than riding over them, which makes its passage both fast and smooth. The vessel is designed to be used by coastal police patrols and special military forces.

Hull shapes

Powerboat hulls are designed to offer little resistance as they move through the water, so that they can reach the highest possible speeds. One way to achieve this is to make a very slim single hull, or monohull, that slices through the waves. A twin-hulled boat, or catamaran, also cuts down the amount of contact between hulls and water, reducing friction. Hydroplanes solve the problem by rising right up out of the water, skimming over the surface with the least drag, or resistance.

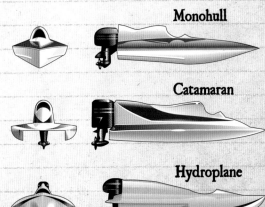

Monohull

Catamaran

Hydroplane

Underwater vessels

Any submarine craft needs a strong hull to withstand the pressure deep underwater and a tube-shaped design to cut through it with least resistance. The largest underwater craft are nuclear submarines with powerful engines that can travel far away from base without refueling. Smaller underwater vessels, known as submersibles, are used for scientific and shipwreck exploration, as well as for checking oil rigs and making repairs below the water.

Country: U.S.
Date: 1800
Size: 21 ft (6.4 m) long
Construction: iron framework, copper outer covering
Top speed: 4 mph (6.5 km/h) underwater
On board: 3

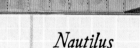

Nautilus

This strange craft was powered by sail on the surface and by a hand-cranked propeller underwater. It was invented by American Robert Fulton, and tested in France, where it stayed underwater for an hour. The aim was to use *Nautilus* to attach explosives to the hulls of enemy ships, but the craft was never used in naval warfare.

Country: U.S.
Date: 1897
Size: 53 ft (16.3 m) long
Construction: iron
Top speed: 9 mph (15 km/h) underwater
On board: 7

Holland No. 6

Irish-American engineer James Holland's *No. 6* was called a "monster war fish" in the American press. It was the first modern submarine, and boasted ballast tanks, torpedo tubes, and a periscope that could be retracted when the craft dived (features that were used on nearly all the later submarines). It had hydroplanes (fins) to help move up and down.

Country: France
Date: 1893
Size: 159 ft (48.5 m) long
Construction: copper
Top speed: 7½ mph (12 km/h) underwater
On board: 19

Gustave Zédé

This was the first submarine to be fitted with a periscope, which allowed the captain and the crew to view the surface of the water while they were still submerged. One of the first effective submarines, this sleek vessel was driven by an electric motor powered by huge batteries.

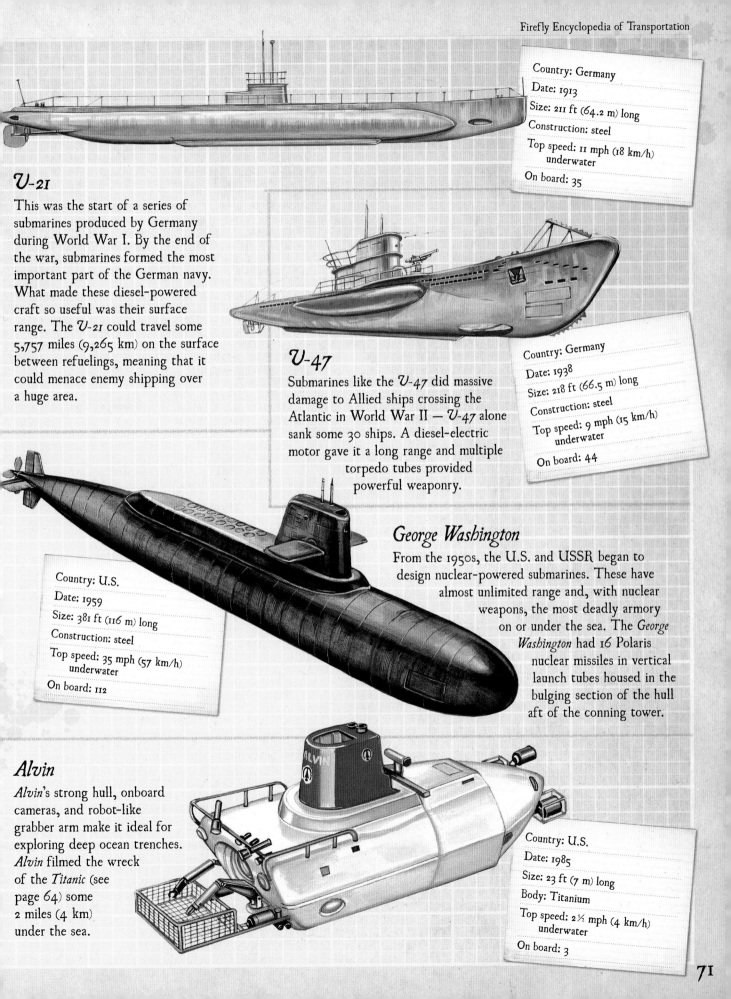

U-21

This was the start of a series of submarines produced by Germany during World War I. By the end of the war, submarines formed the most important part of the German navy. What made these diesel-powered craft so useful was their surface range. The *U-21* could travel some 5,757 miles (9,265 km) on the surface between refuelings, meaning that it could menace enemy shipping over a huge area.

Country: Germany
Date: 1913
Size: 211 ft (64.2 m) long
Construction: steel
Top speed: 11 mph (18 km/h) underwater
On board: 35

U-47

Submarines like the *U-47* did massive damage to Allied ships crossing the Atlantic in World War II — *U-47* alone sank some 30 ships. A diesel-electric motor gave it a long range and multiple torpedo tubes provided powerful weaponry.

Country: Germany
Date: 1938
Size: 218 ft (66.5 m) long
Construction: steel
Top speed: 9 mph (15 km/h) underwater
On board: 44

George Washington

From the 1950s, the U.S. and USSR began to design nuclear-powered submarines. These have almost unlimited range and, with nuclear weapons, the most deadly armory on or under the sea. The *George Washington* had 16 Polaris nuclear missiles in vertical launch tubes housed in the bulging section of the hull aft of the conning tower.

Country: U.S.
Date: 1959
Size: 381 ft (116 m) long
Construction: steel
Top speed: 35 mph (57 km/h) underwater
On board: 112

Alvin

Alvin's strong hull, onboard cameras, and robot-like grabber arm make it ideal for exploring deep ocean trenches. *Alvin* filmed the wreck of the *Titanic* (see page 64) some 2 miles (4 km) under the sea.

Country: U.S.
Date: 1985
Size: 23 ft (7 m) long
Body: Titanium
Top speed: 2½ mph (4 km/h) underwater
On board: 3

Cargo carriers

Ships that carry cargo are called merchant ships, and there are a huge variety of these vessels on the seas today. They range from vast oil tankers to tiny tugs, from car-carrying ferries to ships specially built to recover other damaged ships. They may be slow but they can carry much larger amounts of goods and raw materials than any other form of transportation — and at very low costs — anywhere in the world. Cargo ships have very little superstructure (the part above the main deck level). There is a navigation bridge with funnels, and the engines and crew accommodation below. The rest of the ship holds as much cargo as possible.

Gas tanker

When gases are refrigerated under pressure, they turn to liquid. Large gas tankers, carrying liquid gas in big, spherical tanks, became common during the 1970s. Such tankers can contain up to 4.4 million cubic feet (125,000 m³) of liquid gas. These ships ply the oceans, notably between Australia and Japan.

Country: Netherlands
Date: 1973
Size: 318 ft (97 m) long
Construction: steel
Top speed: 12 mph (22 km/h)
On board: 20

Country: Norway
Date: 1978
Size: 1,475 ft (450 m) long
Construction: steel
Top speed: 14 mph (26 km/h)
On board: 18

Supertanker

The world's largest ships can weigh 550,000 tons (500,000 tonnes) and are so huge that they need a couple of miles to slow down and stop. They carry oil in several vast tanks that have to be separated to prevent the oil surging in heavy seas and possible capsizing.

Container ship

Instead of carrying all sorts of goods of many awkward shapes, container vessels carry 20-ft or 40-ft (6-m or 12-m) long metal containers, which fit exactly onto both ships and trucks. The strong containers are stacked in piles of up to 13 and each container can take as much as 24 tons (21.7 tonnes) of cargo.

Country: Spain
Date: 1974
Size: 300 ft (91 m) long
Construction: steel
Top speed: 14 mph (26 km/h)
On board: 20

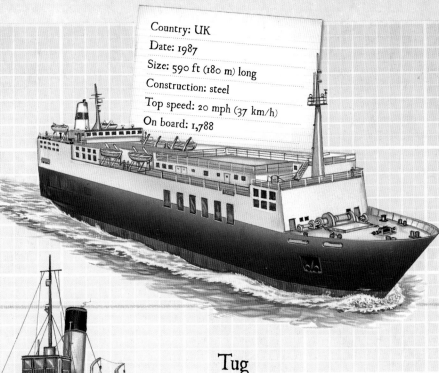

Country: UK
Date: 1987
Size: 590 ft (180 m) long
Construction: steel
Top speed: 20 mph (37 km/h)
On board: 1,788

Ro-ro ferry

Ships that accommodate motor vehicles, allowing you to drive on and off are called "roll-on, roll-off" or ro-ro vessels. They are used widely all over the world to carry all sorts of traffic from trucks loaded with cargo to cars and their passengers. A typical larger ro-ro ship has a series of car decks with access at either end. Above are decks that offer lounges, restaurants and other passenger facilities.

Tug

With the rise of the steam engine, tugs were built to tow sailing ships in and out of port, when the wind was not favorable. Soon tugs were being used for other tasks, such as towing barges, helping large ships to dock, assisting in fire-fighting and helping broken down boats.

Country: France
Date: 1994
Size: 105 ft (32 m) long
Construction: steel
Top speed: 11 mph (20 km/h)
On board: 7

Country: France
Date: 1978
Size: 207 ft (63 m) long
Construction: steel
Top speed: 17 mph (31.5 km/h)
On board: 15

Pontoon barge

How do you transport a damaged ship across the sea? By using a heavy-lift ship called a pontoon barge. It has a long, low deck with tanks that can be filled with water or pumped out. As the barge sinks below sea level, the damaged vessel is floated on board.

Salvage vessel

Ships that have accidents at sea are often brought in by salvage vessels. Such ships are longer and more suited to sailing on the open sea than tugs (which stay close to coasts and ports). For better steering, they may have nozzle-mounted propellers that can be aimed in any direction.

Country: Germany
Date: 1990
Size: 512 ft (156 m) long
Construction: steel
Top speed: 14 ½ mph (27 km/h)
On board: 23

Surface skimmers

For many years, boat builders have realized that if you lift a craft's hull out of the water, you reduce drag, allowing the vessel to travel more quickly. The first vessels to use this idea were hydrofoils, which raise the hull on stilts called foils. A hovercraft works differently, blowing a cushion of air under the hull, so that the craft is just above the water surface. Another design is the catamaran, which has slim twin hulls that lie in the water, and a broad body raised above the surface between the hulls.

Hovercraft *SR.N1*

The hovercraft was invented by British engineer Christopher Cockerell in 1955. Four years later, the first full-size working version impressed onlookers with its speed and its ability to turn on its own axis, and even to reverse.

Country: UK
Date: 1959
Size: 41 ft (12.5 m) long
Construction: steel
Top speed: 70 mph (111 km/h)
On board: 1

Country: UK
Date: 1970 (Mark III model)
Size: 184 ft (56 m) long
Construction: steel, aluminum
Top speed: 70 mph (111 km/h)
On board: 400

Hovercraft *SR.N4*

The original *SR.N4* appeared in 1968 and was the first hovercraft to offer a regular service across the English Channel. By the 1970s, a "stretched" version of the craft was in service, with more space for passengers and cars, and a deep skirt that could cushion the effects of waves at least 15 ft (5 m) high. Passengers like the *SR.N4* because it is fast — at least twice as quick as ordinary ferry boats.

Country: U.S.
Date: 1975
Size: 89 ft (27 m) long
Construction: steel
Top speed: 52 mph (83 km/h)
On board: 240

Flying Dolphin

This is one of the latest hydrofoils used for ferry work between the islands and mainland of Greece. Built in Australia like many vessels of this type, it combines speed, generous passenger space, and comfort. The streamlined hull powers through the water, but when the foils lift it out, drag is reduced still further, allowing the boat to travel even more swiftly.

Country: Australia
Date: 1999
Size: 157 ft (48 m) long
Construction: steel
Top speed: 48 mph (78 km/h)
On board: 516

Boeing Jetfoil

The foils of this craft lift it 6½ ft (2 m) in the air, allowing the Jetfoil to travel more than three times as fast as it can with its hull in the water like a normal boat. The vessel can also tilt like an airplane as it corners, making it more comfortable for those on board.

Country: Japan
Date: 1992
Size: 98 ft (30 m) long
Construction: steel
Top speed: 9 mph (15 km/h)
On board: 3 crew

Yamoto 1

This experimental craft is propelled along by a tube in the water on the underside of the hull. The tube is surrounded by magnets to which an electric current is applied. This pushes the water through the tube at speed, forcing the boat along like a jet engine. The advantage is that the power unit has no moving parts to wear out or go wrong.

Country: Russia
Date: 1998
Size: 39 ft (12 m) long
Construction: aluminum
Top speed: 38 mph (61 km/h)
On board: 8

SeaCat

The SeaCat was the world's first catamaran designed to carry cars. Its twin-hull design is sleeker than ordinary car ferries, meaning that the vessel can skim through the water at speed. But the area between the dual hulls still gives the vessel plenty of breadth, so there is lots of space on board. The ship is powered by water jets and, in addition to the standard 243-ft (74-m) length, a larger SeaCat of 266 ft (81 m) is also in service.

Czilim 20910

Hovercraft are used by modern armed forces for their speed and agility. They can travel rapidly over shallow water or swampland, delivering troops to a trouble spot. This Czilim is a Russian border patrol vessel. The craft's twin diesel engines give it a range of about 300 miles (480 km).

Country: Australia
Date: 1990
Size: 243 ft (74 m) long
Construction: steel
Top speed: 43 mph (69 km/h)
On board: 598

Pleasure craft

People have enjoyed pleasure boating for hundreds of years, but its popularity has increased dramatically since World War II (1939–45). This has been made possible by the use of plywood, fiberglass, and aluminum to make hulls which are tougher, lighter, and cheaper than those made of wooden planking; also by improvements in sail-making and in outboard and inboard motors. More areas of water, such as manmade reservoirs, are also now available for sailing and for speedboats and jet skis.

Windsurfer

Basically a surfboard with a sail, windsurfers have been a popular sporting craft since they first appeared in 1969. Boarders can reach speeds of 50 mph (80 km/h) as they race or jump in competitions.

Country: U.S.
Date: 1999 (this model)
Size: 9 ft (2.7 m) long
Construction: fiberglass
Sail material: artificial fiber
On board: 1

Optimist dinghy

Many children have learned to sail on this type of dinghy, originally designed in 1948. It is small and easy to transport, with a short single mast and a sliding daggerboard keel that allows the shallow hull to sail across the wind.

Country: U.S.
Date: 1980 (this model)
Size: 13 ft (4 m) long
Construction: polyurethane
(high-strength plastic)
Sail material: artificial fiber
On board: 1

Sea Eagle

Inflatable dinghies are among the most versatile of all craft. Boats like this are used by sports divers, for fishing and in rescue work. Because they are so light and very buoyant, they can travel very quickly when fitted with an outboard motor.

Country: U.S.
Date: 1998
Size: 10 ½ ft (3.2 m) long
Construction: reinforced
man-made fiber
Speed: 28 ½ mph (46 km/h)
On board: 5

Jet ski

The "personal watercraft" or jet ski is like a water-borne motorbike and is just as powerful and noisy. A jet ski carries the driver close to the water. Designers are starting to create models that are not so loud, and make less of an impact on the shore environment.

Country: Japan
Date: 1999 (this model)
Size: 9 ft (2.7 m) long
Construction: reinforced fiberglass
Speed: 58 mph (95 km/h)
On board: 2

Country: U.S.

Date: 1988

Size: 27 ft (8.22 m) long

Construction: GRP (glass-reinforced plastic)

Speed: 69 mph (111 km/h)

On board: 4

Country: France

Date: 1998

Size: 31 ft (9.5 m) long

Construction: GRP (glass-reinforced plastic)

Sail material: artificial fiber

On board: 6

Pachanga 27

Powerboats like this Pachanga are tough, lightweight craft built to race at over 60 mph (100 km/h) or to pull water skiers. They have streamlined hulls that ride up out of the water rather than carve their way through it. This is why they can reach high speeds.

Dragonfly 920

The Dragonfly is a trimaran (three-hulled) yacht with outer hulls that can be swung away, giving the boat a narrow beam for towing on the road. The sleek hulls provide plenty of lift, making the boat sail well even upwind and in a light breeze. The carbon-fiber mast combines low weight with high strength.

Country: U.S.

Date: 1997

Size: 30 ft (9.2 m) long

Construction: polyester resin and PVC (polyvinyl chloride, a high-strength plastic)

Sail material: artificial fiber

On board: 4

Oceanis Clipper 311

A cruising yacht can sail on wind power alone but also has a good motor to help make its use safe and flexible. The hull of this vessel accommodates a living area with seating, table, lockers, sleeping berths, a cooking galley and a separate flushing "head" (toilet).

New horizons

Ever since the first boats took to water, the challenge for the adventurous sailor has been to travel faster and farther. The great age of racing began in the 19th century when wealthy enthusiasts started to build yachts especially for this. Racing yachts today use space-age materials for everything from keels to sails, and rely on satellite navigation to find their way. Technological improvements mean people can attempt new feats such as solo around-the-world races, breaking speed records or using mostly muscle power to cross oceans.

The racing powerboat **Miss Britain III** (below) was built in 1933 by boat designer Hubert Scott-Paine. In it, he became the first person to travel at over 100 mph (160 km/h) in a single-engined boat.

Donald Campbell was one of the world's great speed-record breakers. In 1964, driving his hydroplane *Bluebird,* he reached 276¼ mph (444.7 km/h) on Lake Dumbleyung, Australia. He was killed in 1967 when his boat crashed at 320 mph (515 km/h).

Francis Chichester began yacht racing in 1953. By 1960, he had won the first ever solo yacht race across the Atlantic Ocean in his boat **Gipsy Moth III**. He followed up this triumph in 1966–67 with the first solo voyage around the world in *Gipsy Moth IV*, taking a total of 226 days.

The first boat in the grueling Whitbread Round-the-World Race to have an all-woman crew was *Maiden*, a 57-ft (17.5 m) sloop. Many said the 31,980-mile (51,500 km) race was too hard for women but skipper **Tracy Edwards** and her crew proved them wrong. They not only finished the 1989 race but won two of the stages in their class.

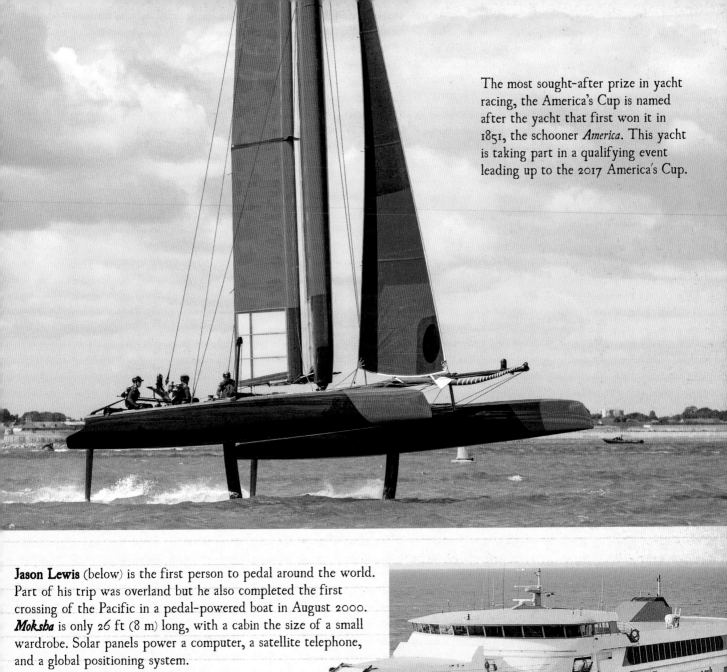

The most sought-after prize in yacht racing, the America's Cup is named after the yacht that first won it in 1851, the schooner *America*. This yacht is taking part in a qualifying event leading up to the 2017 America's Cup.

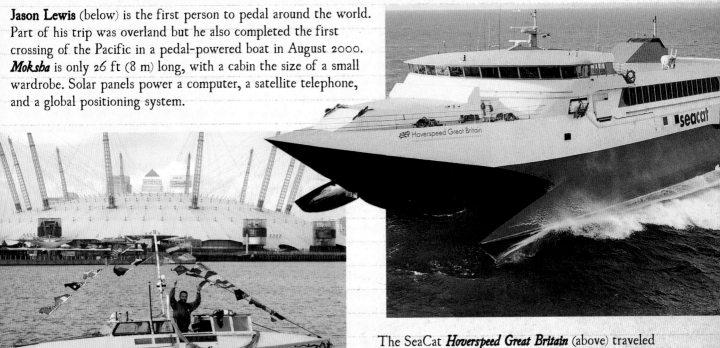

Jason Lewis (below) is the first person to pedal around the world. Part of his trip was overland but he also completed the first crossing of the Pacific in a pedal-powered boat in August 2000. *Moksha* is only 26 ft (8 m) long, with a cabin the size of a small wardrobe. Solar panels power a computer, a satellite telephone, and a global positioning system.

The SeaCat *Hoverspeed Great Britain* (above) traveled across the Atlantic Ocean in 3 days 7 hours and 54 minutes in 1990 — the fastest-ever crossing.

ON THE TRACKS

Railways are the most efficient way to move large numbers of people and heavy cargoes, and they cause the least damage to the environment.

The first railways were simple grooved tracks, carved in stone blocks and used in Babylon in about 2245 BC. Later, horses dragged coal wagons along simple wooden rails until the invention of the steam locomotive 200 years ago. Today a modern freight train hauled by a diesel or electric locomotive can do the same job as over 50 trucks, and a high-speed passenger train can carry the same number of people as 200 cars, in greater comfort and at higher speeds.

The powerful King class steam locomotives, designed in 1927, pulled express trains from London to the west of England for 35 years. *King Edward II* was later rescued from the scrapyard and restored to full working order in a project lasting more than 20 years.

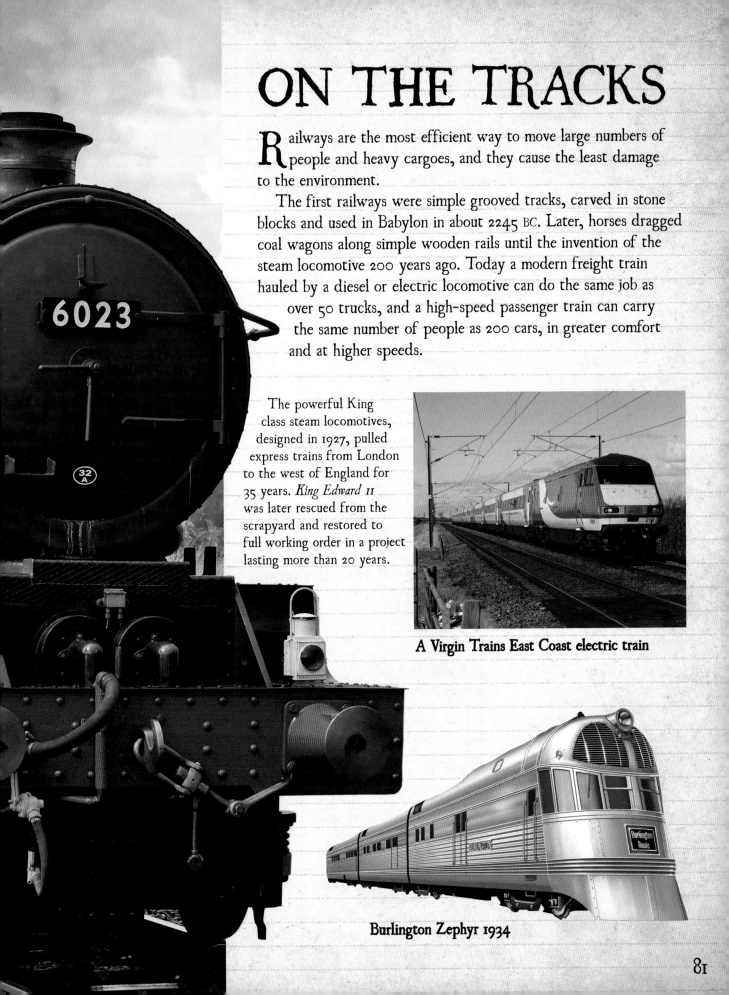

A Virgin Trains East Coast electric train

Burlington Zephyr 1934

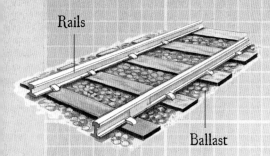

Rails

Ballast

Tracks

Rail tracks are bolted or clipped on to timber, concrete or steel sleepers. These are laid into a track bed of hard stones, which is called ballast.

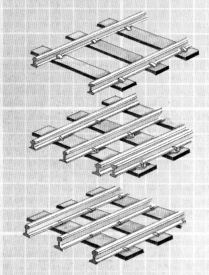

Locomotives ride on two rails, but some electric trains draw their power from a third rail, laid between or alongside the normal tracks.

Power source

Diesel power and electricity took over from steam in the 1950s, offering more power and easier maintenance. A diesel locomotive has an engine positioned between two driving cabs, while the electric draws power from overhead wires or a third rail, and equipment inside converts this into energy to power the wheels.

What is a train?

A train is made up of the locomotive (engine) that pulls the rolling stock (passenger carriages or freight wagons). Trains are powered by electricity, diesel or steam engines, and mostly run on steel rails fixed to the ground. Railways are still the most efficient way to carry large numbers of passengers or huge amounts of goods overland.

Steam locomotive

By the 20th century, steam locomotives were quite complex machines. Coal from the tender at the rear would be shovelled into the firebox, where it was burned to heat the water in the boiler. This is turned into steam, which was forced at high pressure into the cylinders at the front of the engine. Pistons inside the cylinders are connected to long rods that turn the large driving wheels. The trolley of wheels is called a truck (see page 93). The buffers at each end of the locomotive and at the end of the railway track help reduce the shock caused upon contact.

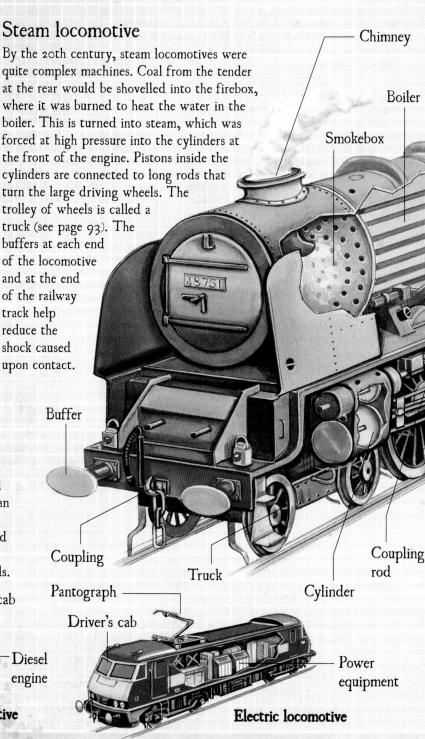

Chimney

Boiler

Smokebox

48751

Buffer

Coupling

Truck

Pantograph

Cylinder

Coupling rod

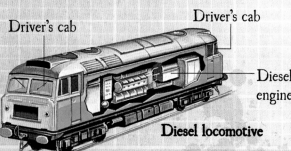

Driver's cab

Driver's cab

Diesel engine

Diesel locomotive

Driver's cab

Power equipment

Electric locomotive

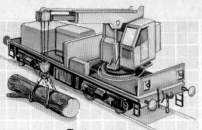

Crane wagon **Snow blower** **Ballast cleaning train**

Types of engine

As well as passenger and freight trains, there are many other types of engines running on the tracks. At nights and on weekends, maintenance crews repair or relay track and check that signals are working properly. Special engineering trains include cranes built on wagons and huge mechanical diggers that clean the ballast (the stones under the track) and ensure the rails are the correct distance apart. Breakdown trains are kept at major depots ready to turn out in an emergency. In winter, snowplows and snowblowers are placed at the front of locomotives to clear the path for trains to run normally.

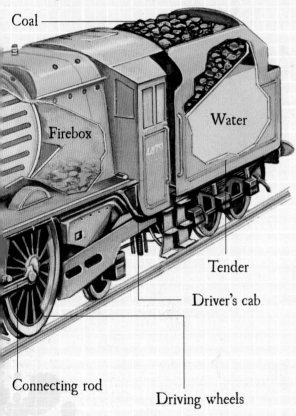

Coal

Firebox

Water

Tender

Driver's cab

Connecting rod

Driving wheels

Driver's cab

While a train is not steered like a car because it travels on fixed rails, the driver still has to operate several levers to keep it moving. The dials on the dashboard indicate speed, the working of the brakes and how much power is being supplied from the diesel engine or electricity source, and alert the driver to faults with carriage lights and automatic doors.

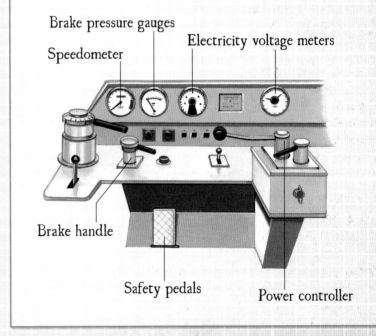

Brake pressure gauges

Speedometer

Electricity voltage meters

Brake handle

Safety pedals

Power controller

Aerodynamics

Like sports cars, trains go faster if they are streamlined. In strong headwinds, the currents sweep effortlessly over the top of a train with a sloping front instead of being trapped, as happens with locomotives with flat front ends. This does not matter much, however, with slow-moving local trains or freights.

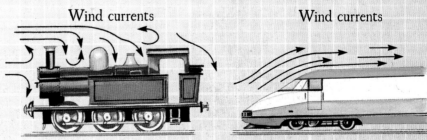

Wind currents

Wind currents

Running on rails

When rails were first laid in stone quarries and coal mines, horses hauled the wagons. However, the wars against Napoleon of France (1799–1815) left Britain with a shortage of these animals. It was the search for a "mechanical horse" that led to the invention of the steam locomotive. From the late 1820s, locomotives were running on tracks in the UK and U.S. By 1840, almost 1,500 miles (2,400 km) of railway had been completed in the UK, and in 1869 a golden spike was driven into the final track of the completed U.S. transcontinental railway.

Trevithick

The world's first steam locomotive to run on rails was built by British engineer Richard Trevithick and ran in 1804 at the Penydarren Ironworks in South Wales. It had flat, tired wheels, and was so heavy that it broke the cast iron rails. But his basic idea of directing the engine's exhaust steam up a chimney became the standard design.

Country: UK
Date: 1804
Size: 15 ft (4.5 m) long
Construction: iron and wood
Top speed: 3 mph (5 km/h)
Number built: 1

Country: UK
Date: 1829
Size: 20 ft (6 m) long
Construction: iron and wood
Top speed: 29 mph (47 km/h)
Number built: 1

Rocket

The Liverpool & Manchester Railway held a competition in 1829 for the best locomotive before it opened in 1830. Robert and George Stephenson's *Rocket* was the winner. It hauled some of the world's very first passenger trains. The design of the *Rocket* also introduced new boiler, exhaust, firebox and simpler drive features that were used in many later steam locomotives.

Locomotion No. 1

George Stephenson designed *Locomotion* for the Stockton & Darlington Railway in 1825. It was the very first engine to have its driving wheels joined together with connecting rods to make sure they turned at the same speed and gave extra grip on slopes.

Country: UK
Date: 1825
Size: 20 ft (6 m) long
Construction: iron and wood
Top speed: 15 mph (24 km/h)
Number built: 1

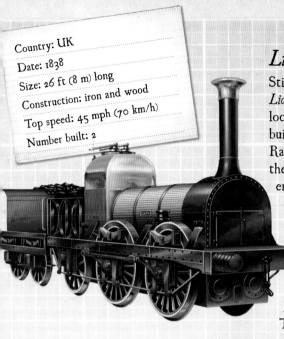

Country: UK
Date: 1838
Size: 26 ft (8 m) long
Construction: iron and wood
Top speed: 45 mph (70 km/h)
Number built: 2

Lion

Still going strong after 160 years, *Lion* is Britain's oldest working locomotive. This six-wheeler was built for the Liverpool & Manchester Railway, and it was rediscovered in the 1920s being used as a pumping engine. Carefully restored to its original condition, it has been used in feature films, including the comedy *The Titfield Thunderbolt*. *Lion* is brought out for special events, and is kept at the Manchester Museum of Science & Technology.

Stirling No. 1

Patrick Stirling, engineer of the Great Northern Railway from 1866 to 1895, was as concerned about how his locomotives looked as he was about how they performed. His *No. 1* was an express engine for the East Coast Main Line, and its single set of driving wheels were an amazing 8 ft (2.5 m) high. *No. 1* became outclassed as trains got longer and heavier, but survives today as one of the most prized exhibits at the National Railway Museum in York.

Country: UK
Date: 1870
Size: 51 ft (16 m) long
Construction: steel
Top speed: 75 mph (120 km/h)
Number built: 53

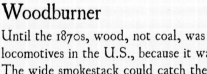

Woodburner

Until the 1870s, wood, not coal, was the fuel of steam locomotives in the U.S., because it was plentiful and cheap. The wide smokestack could catch the hot embers that might cause trackside fires. The "cow-catcher" was a frame at the front to push cattle off the track.

Country: U.S., Canada
Date: 1880
Size: 40 ft (12 m) long
Construction: steel and iron
Top speed: 45 mph (70 km/h)
Number built: over 1,000

Steam-driven trains

Steam locomotives were the dominant form of mass passenger and freight transportation throughout the 19th century and the first half of the 20th century. The trains got streamlined and faster — the American *No. 999* was the first to reach 100 mph (160 km/h). They also grew heavier — "Big Boys" had the strength of 7,000 horses and weighed 550 tons (500 tonnes). But from the 1950s, steam was on the decline.

Country: UK

Date: 1896

Size: 25 ft (8 m) long

Construction: steel

Top speed: 20 mph (30 km/h)

On board: 2 crew

Decapod

As more people had to travel into cities to work, longer and faster trains were needed. The Great Eastern Railway experimented with the Decapod, a monster 10-wheeler that could accelerate away rapidly from the station. But only one was built because it was far too heavy to go over bridges safely.

Country: UK

Date: 1902

Size: 32 ft (10 m) long

Construction: steel

Top speed: 70 mph (110 km/h)

On board: 2 crew

Snowdon Mountain Railway

Rack engines (running on tooth-shape tracks to prevent slipping) began on Mt. Washington, New Hampshire, in 1869. They are a common sight today in the Alps, and in Wales, where this train made the first steep climb to the summit of Mt. Snowdon in 1896.

Garratt

The Garratt was an odd-looking engine that had the boiler in the middle of the engine, with the tank at the front and the coal tender behind. It works like a modern articulated road truck — the main frame has a hinge in the middle to allow it to go around tight curves. Over 2,000 were built in Manchester for export all over the world, and many are still in use in Southern Africa today.

Country: UK

Date: from 1929

Size: 32 ft (10 m) long

Construction: steel

Top speed: 60 mph (37 km/h)

On board: 2 crew

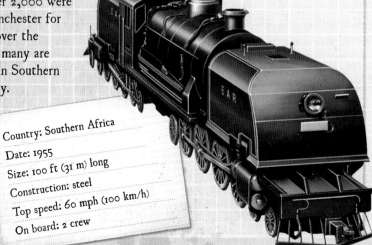

Country: Southern Africa

Date: 1955

Size: 100 ft (31 m) long

Construction: steel

Top speed: 60 mph (100 km/h)

On board: 2 crew

Pannier

Named after the large squared off water tanks slung on both sides of the boiler like panniers on a loaded donkey, the Pannier was the standard small tank engine of the Great Western Railway (GWR). 1,200 were built for use on local passenger and freight trains and for shunting all over the GWR system from London to the west of England and Wales.

"QJ" 0-6-0

One of Britain's ugliest steam engines, the sturdy "QJ" 0-6-0 was built during World War II (1939–45) when there was no money to spend on its appearance. All the working parts were easy to reach, and the "QJ" could haul heavy freight over any route. The first "QJ" is still working in the south of England on a preserved railway.

Country: UK
Date: 1942
Size: 55 ft (17 m) long
Construction: steel
Top speed: 70 mph (45 km/h)
On board: 2 crew

Mallard

The all-time world speed record for steam power was achieved by the streamlined *Mallard* on July 3, 1938. The sloping front end was inspired by the Bugatti racing car and the train reached a top racing speed of 126 mph (202 km/h). The engine is now in the National Railway Museum in York.

Country: UK
Date: 1938
Size: 71 ft (22 m) long
Construction: steel
Top speed: 126 mph (201 km/h)
On board: 2 crew

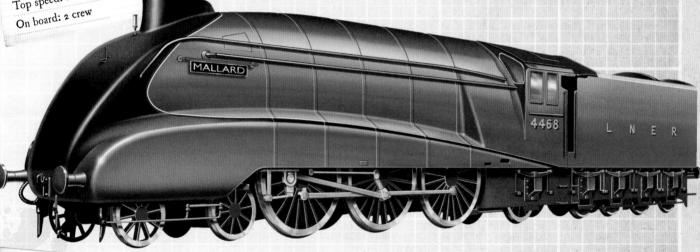

Big Boy

The world's largest steam engines were the massive Big Boys. They were built for the Union Pacific Railroad to haul 4,400-ton (4,000-tonne) freight trains through the Wasatch Mountains in Utah. They stood 16 ft (5 m) high, and had 24 wheels (16 to drive the train).

Country: U.S.
Date: from 1941 to 1956
Size: 131¼ ft (40 m) long
Construction: steel
Top speed: 80 mph (129 km/h)
On board: 2 crew

Diesel-powered trains

Because all their working parts are enclosed inside a large steel box, diesel locomotives tend to look the same all over the world and are not as glamorous as steam trains. But they are cleaner, require less servicing or refueling, and can be easily added to, in order to pull the heaviest transcontinental trains. Diesel engines power generators in the locomotive that provide electricity for the special motors that turn the wheels.

Country: UK
Date: 1948
Size: 61 ft (19 m) long
Construction: steel
Top speed: 93 mph (150 km/h)
On board: 2 crew

10000

The UK's first main line diesel was built as an experiment to compare its performance against the biggest express steam locomotives. The diesel won easily. Looking like American engines, 10000 and its sister 10001 were coupled together and covered almost 1 million miles (1.6 million km).

Country: U.S.
Date: 1934
Size: 196 ft (60 m) long
Construction: steel
Top speed: 104 mph (167 km/h)
On board: 2 crew

Burlington Zephyr

This silver-colored sleek machine was the world's first diesel-electric streamlined train. It was designed to carry the very rich, and made its Denver-to-Chicago run of 1,000 miles (1,600 km) non-stop in 13 hours. There was only room for 50 passengers in the three vehicles that made up the train because of the equipment inside.

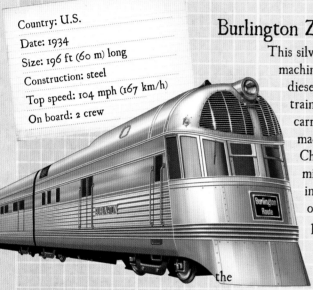

Country: U.S.
Date: 1941
Size: 33 ft (10 m) long
Construction: steel
Top speed: 46 mph (74 km/h)
On board: 2 crew

Deltic

The Deltics packed 3,300 horsepower into their small body making them the world's most powerful diesel-electric locomotive in the 1950s. They were chosen by British Railways to speed up its London-Edinburgh expresses. The original locomotive was painted to look like an American engine.

Whitcomb

Many European countries were desperate for new trains to replace those destroyed during fighting in World War II. American train builder Whitcomb came to the rescue with 200 trains that were so well built, many of them are still working 75 years later. In Italy, they shunt carriages, while in France they are used in factory sidings. Despite their fairly small size, they are both powerful and easy to drive.

Country: UK
Date: 1955
Size: 66 ft (20 m) long
Construction: steel
Top speed: 100 mph (160 km/h)
On board: 2 crew

V200

German designers devised this "diesel hydraulic" locomotive that had an automatic gearbox and a complicated series of drive shafts to transfer the power from the engine to turn the wheels. Despite looking sharp and being reliable, it was very complicated and expensive to run, and only lasted in service for 20 years. Similar engines ran in Britain too.

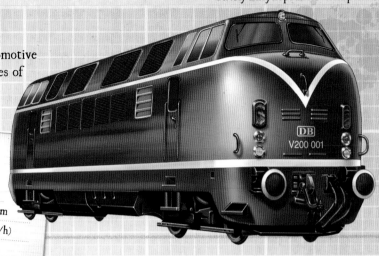

Country: Germany
Date: 1953
Size: 50 ft (15 m) long
Construction: steel, aluminum
Top speed: 75 mph (120 km/h)
On board: 2 crew

M62

Russia built over 5,000 of the M62 diesels for use at home and abroad. However, many of those sent to East European countries have been scrapped because they are worn out and unreliable. Their engines smoked so badly that station staff said they needed to wear gas masks when an M62 arrived. Also, M62s cannot haul passenger coaches in winter because they have no heating equipment.

Country: Russia, Hungary
Date: 1965
Size: 57 ft (18 m) long
Construction: steel
Top speed: 60 mph (100 km/h)
On board: 2 crew

SD40-2

Although it is rather noisy, the SD40-2 is regarded as the most reliable heavy-duty diesel locomotive ever built, and many hundreds can be seen around the world. Colors and marking vary depending on which company owns it. In the U.S., their home country, three or four of them are often coupled together to haul freight trains that can be over two miles (3.2 km) long.

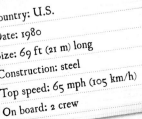

Country: U.S.
Date: 1980
Size: 69 ft (21 m) long
Construction: steel
Top speed: 65 mph (105 km/h)
On board: 2 crew

Electric trains

An electric train picks up power from an overhead wire through a pantograph (a folding arm fixed to the roof), or from an electrified third rail laid alongside the track the train is running on. An electric motor either inside the locomotive or underneath the carriage turns the driving wheels. Trains driven by electricity are more powerful than diesel and steam, and accelerate much faster. Electricity is also a cleaner fuel.

Country: UK
Date: from 1904
Size: 53 ft (16 m) long
Construction: steel
Top speed: 90 mph (145 km/h)
On board: 2 crew

Early electric

The UK's first electric locomotives were built by the North Eastern Railway to haul coal around the Newcastle area. They only ran for 20 years because they were too complicated and expensive to run. Coal was still very cheap to buy, so the NER went back to steam trains.

Country: Switzerland/Austria
Date: from 1919
Size: 27 ft (17 m) long
Construction: steel
Top speed: 80 mph (130 km/h)
On board: 2 crew

Crocodile

Some of the earliest electric locomotives built for the Swiss and Austrian Railways were nicknamed "crocodiles" because they had a long, narrow snout with two eyes above it (the cab windows). They were extremely powerful articulated engines, designed to haul heavy goods trains on the steep inclines, sharp curves, and mountain tunnels of the Alps.

Country: U.S.
Date: from 1935
Size: 80 ft (25 m) long
Construction: steel
Top speed: 100 mph (160 km/h)
On board: 2 crew

Metropolitan

The Metropolitan Railway was the first in the UK to use electric locomotives on some passenger trains. It was part of the Underground system and used the same third rail power supply. Twenty of these locomotives were built in the early 1920s and in regular service until 1961. One of them named, *Sarah Siddons*, has been kept in working order by London Underground for special runs.

Country: UK
Date: from 1922
Size: 40 ft (12 m) long
Construction: steel
Top speed: 65 mph (105 km/h)
On board: 2 crew

GG1

American railway companies always built things to last, and the streamline GG1 Class electrics worked for over 50 years. Designed by a Frenchman, they hauled 14 passenger carriages and heavy freights along the eastern seaboard.

CC7102

In March 1955, SNCF (the French Railways) wanted to see just how fast an electric locomotive could safely go. It chose a plain working train (CC7102) and another (BB9004) for tests. Each train was fitted with a special streamlined front end to improve wind resistance. The engines both reached a still unbeaten record speed of 205½ mph (331.5 km/h).

Country: France
Date: 1952
Size: 62 ft (19 m) long
Construction: steel
Top speed: 87 mph (140 km/h) on standard working models
On board: 2 crew

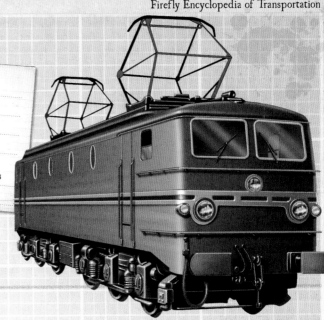

Country: Germany
Date: from 1996
Size: 62 ft (19 m) long
Construction: steel
Top speed: 135 mph (220 km/h)
On board: 2 crew

Class 101

The latest German electric locomotives are giants. They can haul 2,750-ton (2,500-tonne) freight trains at 160 km/h (100 mph), or 14 passenger coaches. It is common for them to travel 1,000 miles (1,600 km) in a single day. The locomotive is filled with computer-controls and can be started in a few seconds. A control center warns the driver of hazards.

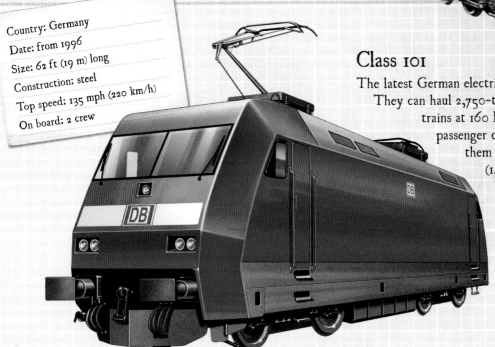

Hitachi Super Express Train

The next generation of express trains in the UK use bi-mode technology to provide a faster service more efficiently. Each train picks up electric power from overhead wires but also has a diesel engine on board for use on non-electrified sections. When the Great Western main line is electrified, this means that the new express trains can continue beyond the limit of the wires to more destinations without the high cost of full network electrification.

Country: UK, Japan
Date: 2014
Size: 5 or 10 coach trains
Construction: steel
Top speed: 125 mph (200 km/h)

TEE Express (Europe)

Pendolino (Italy)

Bullet Train (Japan)

High-speed trains

High-speed trains are vital for the future of the railways. The TGV, ICE, Eurostar, Japanese Bullet Train, and other super express trains have won back many passengers who normally travel long distances between major cities by air. Cruising speeds of 155 mph (250 km/h) and higher have cut rail journey times, while improved track, suspension systems and soundproofing give a more comfortable ride. But while some new high-speed rail services have been introduced in most western European countries as well as Russia and China, there are few fast passenger trains in the U.S. The UK's second high-speed line (HS2) is not due to open before 2026.

The Beijing–Guangzhou high-speed railway is the longest in the world, at 1,428 miles (2,298 km). Its bullet trains have an average speed of 155 mph (250 km/h).

Tilting mechanism

Some modern trains have special tilt devices to allow them to travel at high speeds along curves. The train tilts by means of a hydraulic system. This mechanism causes the train to adjust itself to the curves by tilting its body in relation to the trucks (see page 93). The train can then safely cover existing rail track curves at far higher speeds than conventional trains. The Virgin Pendolinos used on the west coast main line between London and Glasgow are all tilting trains.

Normal   Tiltline

Driver's cab

Streamlined shape

Headlights

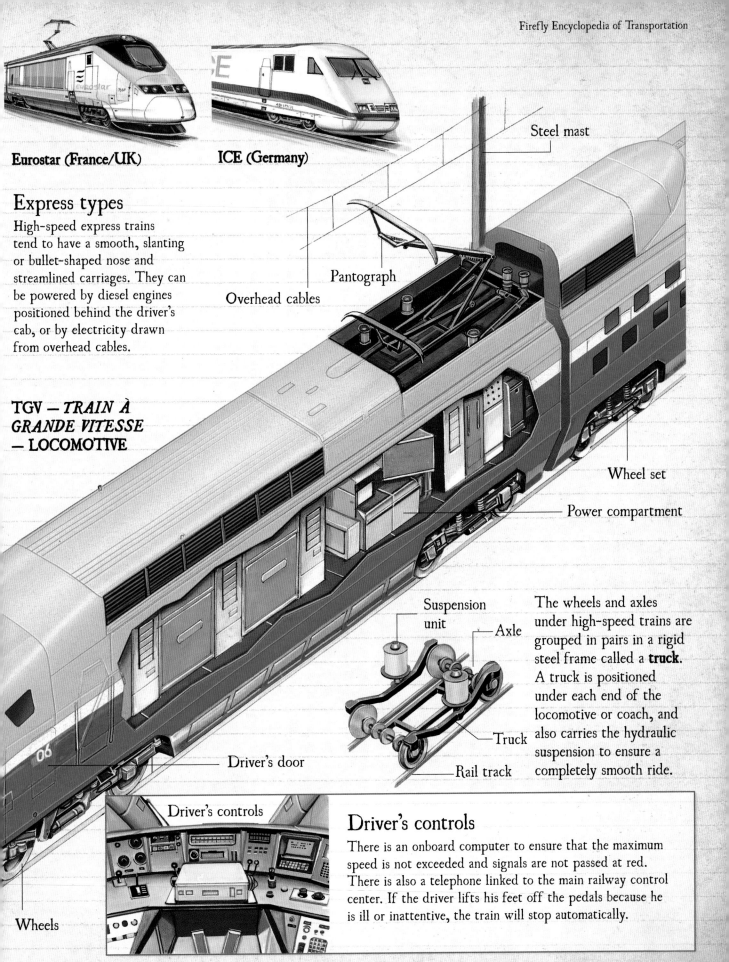

Eurostar (France/UK)

ICE (Germany)

Express types

High-speed express trains tend to have a smooth, slanting or bullet-shaped nose and streamlined carriages. They can be powered by diesel engines positioned behind the driver's cab, or by electricity drawn from overhead cables.

TGV – *TRAIN À GRANDE VITESSE* – LOCOMOTIVE

Steel mast

Pantograph

Overhead cables

Wheel set

Power compartment

Suspension unit

Axle

Truck

Rail track

The wheels and axles under high-speed trains are grouped in pairs in a rigid steel frame called a **truck**. A truck is positioned under each end of the locomotive or coach, and also carries the hydraulic suspension to ensure a completely smooth ride.

Driver's door

Driver's controls

Wheels

Driver's controls

There is an onboard computer to ensure that the maximum speed is not exceeded and signals are not passed at red. There is also a telephone linked to the main railway control center. If the driver lifts his feet off the pedals because he is ill or inattentive, the train will stop automatically.

Around the world on rail

By the end of World War I (1914–18) there were about 1 million miles (1.6 million km) of rail routes, a quarter of which were in the United States. Rail had become the most widely used machine-assisted transportation around the world. Great engineering feats of the 20th century, such as the Trans-Siberian Railroad, are still heavily used today, while many modern trains can carry 1,000 passengers or haul thousands of tons of freight cargo across continents.

Robinson 2-8-0

Hundreds of these cheap but strong British freight steam engines were exported all over the world to move supplies and soldiers during wars. They were camouflaged to make them harder to spot by enemy planes.

Country: UK

Date: 1914

Size: 62 ft (19 m) long

Construction: steel

Top speed: 60 mph (100 km/h)

On board: 2 crew

Flying Scotsman

The powerful A3 Pacific Class locomotives were used on the east coast main line from London to Edinburgh, including the famous nonstop express train, the *Flying Scotsman*. In a 40-year working life, the engine covered over 3 million miles (4.75 million km). It has now been restored to full working order by the National Railway Museum for use on special excursion trips. It remains one of the most famous locomotives ever built.

Country: UK

Date: 1923

Size: 70 ft (22 m) long

Construction: steel

Top speed: 100 mph (160 km/h)

On board: 2 crew

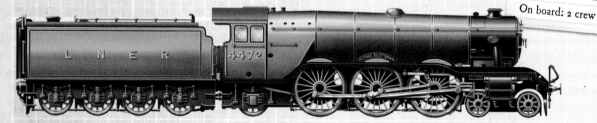

Pullman

American George Mortimer Pullman (1831–97) built luxury passenger coaches that today are known as Pullmans. Railway companies paid to use these carriages as early as 1875, and the British *Brighton Belle* electric trains used them until 1972. Many of these hotels-on-wheels have been restored for the Orient Express service run by Venice Simplon Orient Express (VSOE).

Country: worldwide

Date: 1932

Size: 320 ft (100 m) long

Construction: steel

Top speed: 90 mph (145 km/h)

On board: 152 passengers

Country: Russia
Date: 1954
Size: 90 ft (28 m) long
Construction: steel
Top speed: 75 mph (120 km/h)
On board: 2 crew

Trans-Siberian

The Trans-Siberian Express takes nine days to travel the 5,777 miles (9,297 km) between Moscow and Vladivostock, making it the world's longest single train journey. The line was completed in 1905 and was then the world's most northerly track. Today it uses both diesel and electric trains.

Canadian Pacific

The Canadian Pacific Railway (renamed Canadian National) runs from the east to the west coast of Canada. Passenger trains take three days to cover the 2,880-mile (4,634-km) journey from Montreal to Vancouver. They are often over 20 coaches long, and run past lakes and through prairie country before making the steep climb into the Rocky Mountains.

Country: Canada
Date: 1955
Size: 1,600 ft (1,000 m) long
Construction: steel
Top speed: 65 mph (100 km/h)
On board: 700 passengers

Blue Train

South Africa has two Blue Trains for its 1,000-mile (1,600 km) journey from Pretoria to Cape Town. (Some also go to Victoria Falls.) They have 18 carriages offering the world's most luxurious passenger service with private bedrooms and bathrooms.

Country: South Africa
Date: 1972
Size: 1,000 ft (620 m) long
Construction: steel
Top speed: 50 mph (80 km/h)
On board: 100 passengers

Australian long haul

The Hammersley Iron Company runs trains with up to 210 wagons, each loaded with over 110 tons (100 tonnes) of ore. Three locomotives are needed to get them moving. Along the route is the world's longest continuous stretch of straight track — 297 miles (478 km) across the Australian Nullabor Plain.

Country: Australia
Date: 1980s
Size: ½ mile (1 km) long
Construction: steel
Top speed: 55 mph (90 km/h)
On board: 2 crew

Carrying goods by rail

In the days before huge articulated trucks, lots of smaller trains carried all sorts of smaller items of goods. Today, goods carried by rail tend to be bulk raw items such as coal or sand in open wagons, or liquefied gas carried in insulated wagons. Large manufactured products such as cars are also commonly transported by freight trains, usually on double-tier wagons.

Old style coal wagon

The railways once made far more money transporting coal than carrying passengers. Coal was loaded into wagons with simple wooden sides, no roof, and primitive brakes. Sometimes 50 wagons were made up into one train.

Country: worldwide
Date: from 1850
Size: 16 ft (5 m) long
Construction: steel, wood
Top speed: 50 mph (80 km/h)
Number built: millions
On board: 0

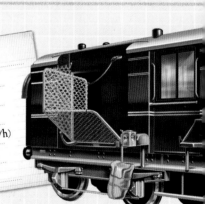

Brake van

Freight trains used to have brake vans in which the guard sat in a special wooden observation coach coupled to the end of the wagons. His job was to keep an eye on wagons whose brakes were sticking, or even spilling their load.

Country: UK
Date: 1949
Size: 27 ft (8 m) long
Construction: steel, wood
Top speed: 65 mph (100 km/h)
Number built: 1,250
On board: 1 guard

Merry-go-round

Coal-fired power stations, now being replaced by other fuel sources, have been supplied for over 50 years by "merry-go-round" trains, so called because each coal train never stops moving to unload. As it travels slowly past the unloading area, a lever opens a door on the bottom of each wagon to release the coal straight onto a conveyor belt and into the furnace.

Country: UK
Date: from 1929
Size: 60 ft (18 m) long
Construction: steel
Top speed: 75 mph (120 km/h)
Number built: 68
On board: 20 sorters

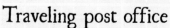

Traveling post office

Postmen used to travel on mail trains to sort letters and parcels before they arrived at their destination. Bags of mail waiting to be sorted were hung on a large net attached to a steel frame on the side of the track and snatched into the train at high speed.

Country: UK
Date: 1965
Size: 20 ft (6 m) long
Construction: steel
Top speed: 50 mph (75 km/h)
Number built: over 1,000
On board: 2 crew

Car carrier

Brand new cars can be moved by rail direct from the factory to a ship or a showroom in special wagons known as transporters. Up to 100 cars can be moved in one trip, often stacked in two tiers. Larger vans and trucks are placed on low trucks to avoid hitting any bridges. Britain alone once had about 20,000 of these carriers.

Country: worldwide

Date: from 1965

Size: 80 ft (24 m) long

Construction: steel

Top speed: 75 mph (120 km/h)

On board: 2 crew

Country: U.S.

Date: 1960

Size: 100 ft (30 m)

Construction: steel

Top speed: 60 mph (100 km/h)

On board: 2 crew

Double stack containers

There are few bridges on American long-distance railways, so it is possible to stack containers two-high on special flat freight wagons. Powerful diesels can haul trains of up to 2 miles (3.2 km) long, which can mean a half-hour wait at level crossings as they pass through. A crane lifts the container onto a waiting truck or directly into the hold of a ship.

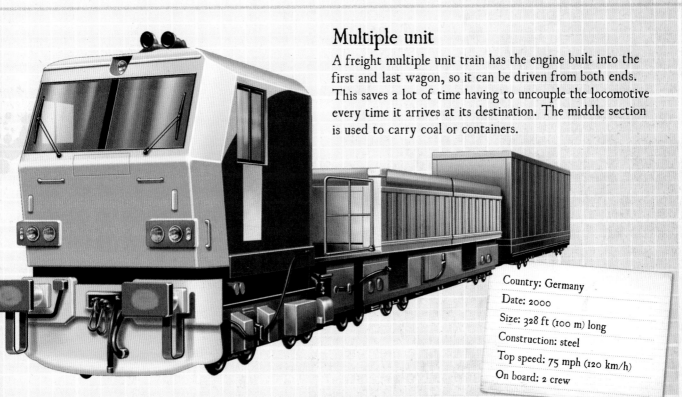

Multiple unit

A freight multiple unit train has the engine built into the first and last wagon, so it can be driven from both ends. This saves a lot of time having to uncouple the locomotive every time it arrives at its destination. The middle section is used to carry coal or containers.

Country: Germany

Date: 2000

Size: 328 ft (100 m) long

Construction: steel

Top speed: 75 mph (120 km/h)

On board: 2 crew

Traveling underground

Big cities need public transportation to move large numbers of people around, and often this mode of transportation is hidden underground to keep travelers away from roads and save valuable building space. Up to 50,000 people can be moved in one direction every hour, at speeds of 10 to 50 mph (16 to 80 km/h) and often without the delays transportation has above ground. Most underground trains are electric and get their power from a third rail. The first passenger-carrying underground line was the Metropolitan Railway in London, opened in 1863. This gave its name to city systems around the world, which are usually called Metros.

Metropolitan No. 23

Although it is now all-electric, the London Underground started with steam trains. No. 23 is the only surviving locomotive from the world's first underground railway, now preserved in the London Transport Museum. Large pipes took the steam from the cylinders and condensed it into cold water tanks. This was an attempt to reduce exhaust fumes in the tunnels but the atmosphere on the Underground before electrification in 1905 was pretty unpleasant!

Country: UK
Date: 1866
Size: 33 ft (10 m) long
Construction: steel
Top speed: 50 mph (80 km/h)
On board: 2 crew

Country: France
Date: from 1960
Size: 66 ft (20 m) long
Construction: steel, aluminum
Top speed: 35 mph (55 km/h)
On board: 80 per coach

Paris Metro

Over 260 miles (400 km) of rail lines thread their way underneath France's capital city, serving over 450 stations. Many of the trains are fitted with rubber tires that give a much quieter and more comfortable ride than conventional steel wheels. Over 1,500 million passengers a year ride on the Paris Metro, with over 4,500 coaches in daily service.

Country: U.S.
Date: from 1950
Size: 75 ft (23 m) long
Construction: steel
Top speed: 50 mph (80 km/h)
On board: 80 per coach

New York subway

With 25 separate lines and 469 stations, the New York subway is one of the busiest in the world. Over 1,000 million people a year buy a subway ticket. Most of the famous old trains, which were noisy, shabby, uncomfortable and plastered with graffiti, are being replaced by new stock.

Country: UK

Date: from 1977

Size: 42 ft (13 m) long

Construction: steel

Top speed: 34 mph (54 km/h)

On board: 36 per coach

"Clockwork Orange"

Trains on the Glasgow Underground are nicknamed "Clockwork Oranges" because of their bright color (and after a well-known novel and film of the same name). Formed of several coaches coupled together, they run in a circle under the city center, going under the River Clyde twice.

San Francisco BART

There are 700 fully automatic BART (Bay Area Rapid Transit) trains running on special wide tracks around San Francisco in California. They have a strange lopsided, one-eyed appearance because the driver only has one front window. The 3½-mile (5.8-km) tunnel to Oakland is the longest underwater rail tunnel in the U.S.

Country: U.S.

Date: 1972

Size: 75 ft (23 m) long

Construction: steel

Top speed: 50 mph (80 km/h)

On board: 100

Country: China

Date: 1998

Size: 42 ft (13 m) long

Construction: steel, aluminum

Top speed: 85 mph (125 km/h)

On board: 60 per coach

Hong Kong Metro

Millions of tons of earth had to be moved to make room for the new fully automatic section of this metro linking the island city to its modern Chinese airport. A seven-car metro leaves the airport platform every three minutes.

Country: China

Date: 1998

Size: 42 ft (13 m) long

Construction: steel

Top speed: 50 mph (80 km/h)

On board: 100 per coach

Guangzhou Metro

Metro construction in mainland China took off with the country's rapid economic growth in the 1990s. Guangzhou, the country's third largest city, opened its first metro line in 1998 with these trains supplied by Siemens-AEG from Germany. Guangzhou now has eight lines with six more under way. Since 2000 new metros have opened in more than 20 booming Chinese cities.

Light rail

Light rail is the term now used to describe tramways, which have had a revival in cities all over the world since the 1980s. Tramways first took off in American cities in the 1850s, when it was found that horses could pull a much larger and heavier vehicle on smooth iron rails instead of a rough road surface. By the 1890s, trams were being mechanized, first with cable haulage, then with electricity, bringing fast, cheap public transportation to towns and cities everywhere. The more flexible motor bus began to replace trams in the mid-1900s but today its environmental benefits and ability to move huge crowds quickly in cities polluted and congested by cars and buses has put the modern electric tram back on the streets.

Country: Germany

Date: 1960

Size: 40 ft (25 m) long

Construction: steel

Top speed: 40 mph (65 km/h)

On board: 150+ passengers

Country: UK

Date: from 1900

Size: 36 ft (11 m) long

Construction: steel, wood

Top speed: 30 mph (50 km/h)

On board: 55 passengers

British electric tram

In the early 1900s, there were double-deck trams like this in most British cities. They ran on rails in the street, picking up power from an overhead electric wire. By the 1960s, traditional trams had nearly all been replaced by diesel buses but, since 1992, six completely new light rail systems with European-built single deck trams have opened in the UK.

European tram

While UK cities all replaced their electric trams, many towns in Europe kept their systems and are replacing these sturdy traditional trams with modern light rail vehicles. European trams have always been single deck but are often articulated or coupled together to carry large numbers. Several completely new urban tram networks have been developed since the 1980s, notably in France.

Country: U.S.

Date: 2003

Size: 87 ft (26.5 m) long twin unit

Construction: steel, aluminum

Top speed: 55 mph (89 km/h)

Los Angeles metro

Los Angeles, a city long dominated by private cars, has opened four light rail lines since 1990 to improve its public transportation. The Gold Line, first opened in 2003, links LA with Pasadena. The current trains are similar to European style electric trams and were built in Italy by AnsaldoBreda. They are articulated two-car units that can be coupled together to make a train.

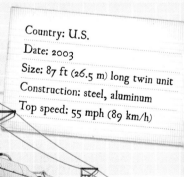

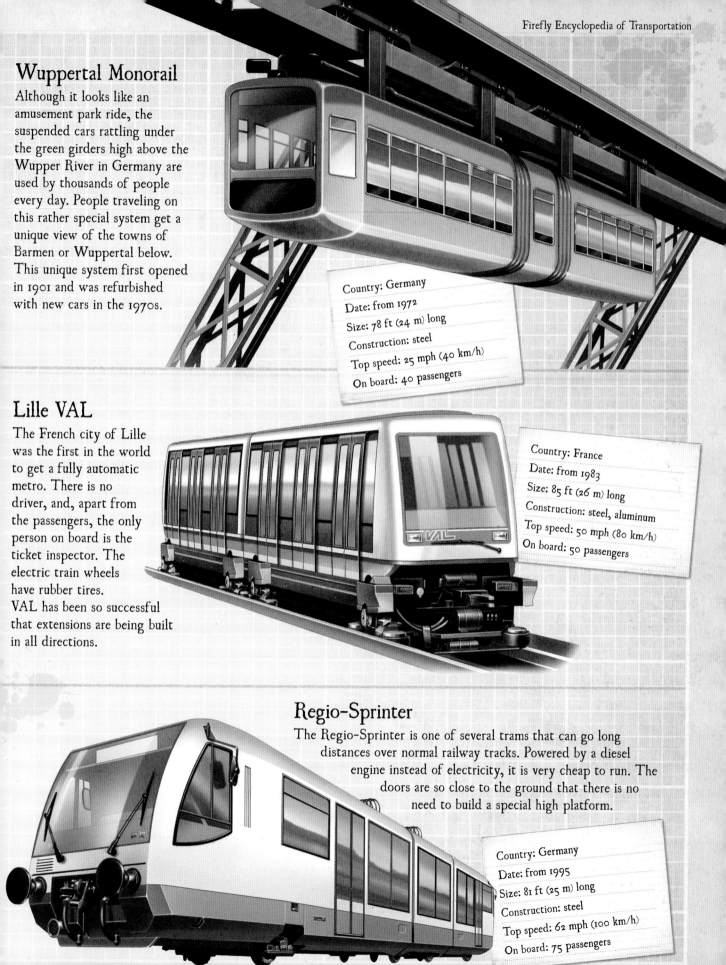

Wuppertal Monorail

Although it looks like an amusement park ride, the suspended cars rattling under the green girders high above the Wupper River in Germany are used by thousands of people every day. People traveling on this rather special system get a unique view of the towns of Barmen or Wuppertal below. This unique system first opened in 1901 and was refurbished with new cars in the 1970s.

Country: Germany

Date: from 1972

Size: 78 ft (24 m) long

Construction: steel

Top speed: 25 mph (40 km/h)

On board: 40 passengers

Lille VAL

The French city of Lille was the first in the world to get a fully automatic metro. There is no driver, and, apart from the passengers, the only person on board is the ticket inspector. The electric train wheels have rubber tires. VAL has been so successful that extensions are being built in all directions.

Country: France

Date: from 1983

Size: 85 ft (26 m) long

Construction: steel, aluminum

Top speed: 50 mph (80 km/h)

On board: 50 passengers

Regio-Sprinter

The Regio-Sprinter is one of several trams that can go long distances over normal railway tracks. Powered by a diesel engine instead of electricity, it is very cheap to run. The doors are so close to the ground that there is no need to build a special high platform.

Country: Germany

Date: from 1995

Size: 81 ft (25 m) long

Construction: steel

Top speed: 62 mph (100 km/h)

On board: 75 passengers

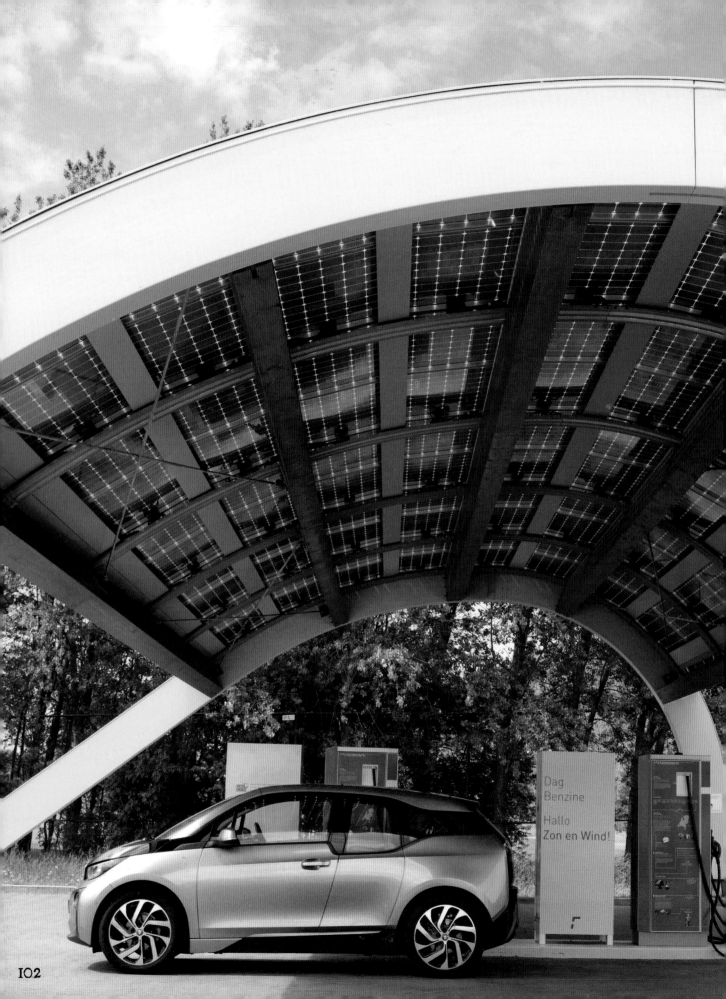

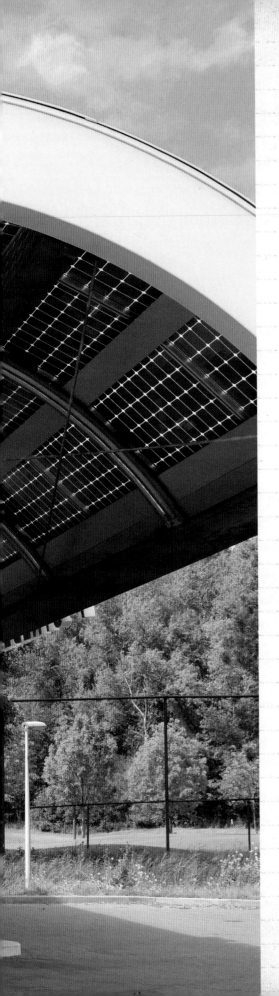

GREENER TRANSPORTATION

Government estimates in the U.S. and the UK suggest that transportation of all kinds accounts for around a quarter of greenhouse gas emissions. More than half of these come from personal vehicles including cars, pickup trucks and SUVs. In the U.S., greater demand for travel and cheap fuel has led to a 35 percent rise in vehicle miles traveled since 1990. Car use has also risen dramatically across the world, particularly in Europe and China.

This is affecting air quality in the cities where most of us live and is contributing to climate change. Low-emission vehicles, new technologies and innovative forms of transportation are being developed to encourage a move to cleaner, greener ways of getting around. We need to reduce our dependence on fossil fuels such as coal, oil and petroleum, and develop renewable sources of energy for our future transportation.

While technological advances continue to produce more environmentally friendly vehicles such as **solar cars** (*below*), the greenest form of transportation continues to be walking or cycling.

As increasing numbers of electric cars hit the roads, more **charging stations** are being built. This fast-charging station in the Netherlands is powered by solar panels on its roof and can recharge a car in under half an hour.

Green machines

It is now generally accepted that carbon dioxide and other greenhouse gas emissions from burning fossil fuels such as coal, gas and oil are contributing to global warming and climate change. Many of these damaging emissions come from road vehicles and planes. Since the 1990s, there has been a lot of research into the development of greener transportation methods that cause less pollution and use different forms of renewable energy.

Ford Escape New York City taxi

The Ford Escape Hybrid was the first American-built gas–electric hybrid vehicle. Its drive system can switch automatically between pure battery electric power, pure gas power, or a combination of the two, working together for maximum power and fuel efficiency. From 2005, New York City began using the Escape Hybrid as a taxicab, painted in the familiar bright yellow of U.S. cabs.

Toyota Prius

The Toyota Prius was the first mass-produced hybrid car, launched in 1997. It has two power sources, a normal gas engine and a battery electric motor drive, which saves on fuel and cuts down polluting emissions. By 2015 more than 5.2 million cars had been sold around the world. It is still rated as one of the cleanest vehicles sold in the U.S., based on smog-forming emissions, and has one of the best fuel economy records.

Country: Japan
Introduced : 1997
Power: gas/electric hybrid
On board: 4

Country: U.S.
Date: 2005
Size: 14 ft 7 in. (4.44 m) long
Power: gas/electric hybrid
Construction: steel
On board: driver + 4 passengers

Country: Belgium
Introduced: 2003
Size: 57 ft 8 in. (17.58 m) long
Top speed: 40 mph (65 km/h)
Construction: steel
On board: 45 seated + 100 standing

Van Hool articulated trolleybus

Modern trolleybuses look like conventional single-deck motor buses except for the twin trolley poles on the roof that run along electrified overhead wires. This is an all-electric, high-capacity articulated trolleybus supplied to Athens, Greece in the run-up to the 2004 Olympics. The city has very poor air quality and decided to expand its clean electric public transportation system rather than buying more polluting diesel buses.

Shanghai Airport Maglev

The Shanghai Airport Maglev is the fastest commercial train in the world. It works by magnetic levitation (maglev), based on the basic law of magnetism that like poles repel each other while opposite poles attract. The special guideway has a set of magnetized coils running along it. When electrically powered up, these repel a set of large magnets on the underside of the train, making it levitate just over the guideway as it moves along. With no friction through physical contact, it can travel efficiently at very high speeds.

Country: China/Germany
Introduced: 2004
Size: 500 ft (153 m) long
Power: electricity
Top speed: 270 mph (430 km/h)
Construction: steel
On board: 574 passengers

Wrightbus New Routemaster London bus

This diesel–electric hybrid has a diesel engine that runs only when the battery for the electric motor needs charging, so the bus has lower emissions and more economical and efficient fuel consumption than earlier double-deckers. The stylish retro design, by Heatherwick Studio, brings back the look and comfort of the much-loved 1950s Routemaster but with full accessibility and more seating. It has three doors, two staircases and a climate-controlled ventilation system.

Country: UK
Date: 2012
Size: 36 ft 10 in. (11.23 m) long
Power: diesel–electric hybrid
On board: driver/conductor + 80 passengers

Nissan Leaf

The Nissan Leaf is the world's best-selling all-electric car. Electric cars have been made since the 1880s but have only become mass-produced in the 21st century with growing concern about air pollution and greenhouse gas emissions from gasoline engines. The Leaf is powered entirely by rechargeable batteries, and produces no tailpipe emissions. On full charge, it has a range of up to 120 miles (200 km), making it ideal as a short-distance city car.

Country: Japan
Date: 2010
Size: 14 ft 5 in. (4.4 m) long
Body: steel
Top speed: 93 mph (150 km/h) depending on model
On board: 4

How a hydrogen fuel cell bus works

One of the most promising new technologies being applied to transportation is the hydrogen fuel cell, which can be used to power an electric motor on a vehicle. A fuel cell bus uses compressed hydrogen, carried in tanks, as fuel. When combined with oxygen in onboard fuel cells, the reaction creates mechanical energy to run the vehicle's electric motors. The great environmental benefit of this is that there are no harmful emissions. With no engine, this bus is very quiet and the only emission from the power source is water vapor. Fuel cell buses are being tested by several manufacturers in cities across the world. As the technology is refined, the high cost of these green machines will come down. This could be the bus of the future.

Greener cities

London has the largest bus fleet in the world and is committed to reducing pollution levels on its busy roads. Since 2004 a series of hydrogen fuel cell buses have been tested on a city center route that crosses Tower Bridge. London is a major partner in the Clean Hydrogen in European Cities (CHIC) project, which has brought fuel cell buses and refueling stations to a number of cities across Italy, Switzerland, Germany and Norway, and assesses the environmental, economic and social impact of this new technology.

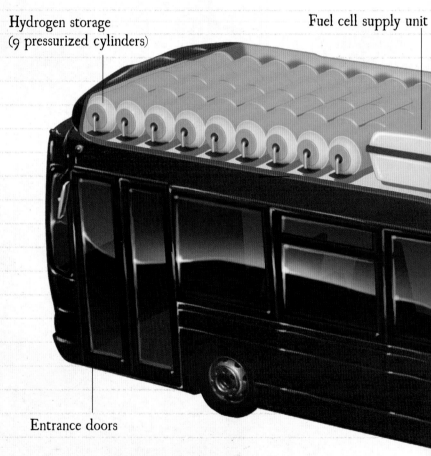

Hydrogen storage
(9 pressurized cylinders)

Fuel cell supply unit

Entrance doors

Passenger
exit doors

Hydrogen fueling stations are needed to refuel hydrogen fuel cell buses and cars. As the technology becomes more popular and affordable, more fueling stations are being built worldwide.

These **hydrogen fuel cell–electric hybrid coaches** were used to transport visitors to the 2005 World Expo in Aichi, Japan. The Expo allowed visitors to experience cutting-edge technology using renewable energies.

Fuel cell stacks for converting hydrogen into energy

Hydraulic fans for cooling the fuel cell stacks

Air-conditioning unit maintains a comfortable temperature inside the bus

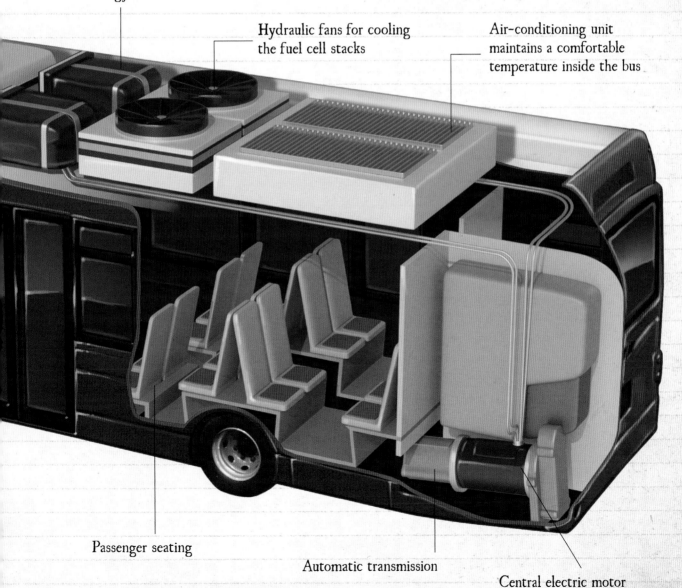

Passenger seating

Automatic transmission

Central electric motor

Running on empty

With fuel supplies dwindling and cities getting more polluted from vehicle exhaust emissions, the search is on for forms of transportation that use less fossil fuel energy. Car makers have produced "hybrid" cars that run on both electricity and gasoline. The power of the sun could offer another solution, and there are already some exciting experimental cars and boats. In the future, you may drive a hydrogen- or solar-powered car. It may even drive you as the technology of robotic "autonomous" vehicles is developed.

When fog and pollutants, such as exhaust fumes, get mixed up in cities, they create **smog**. This damages health and the atmosphere.

Going forward

Concept cars do not often make it to volume production. The **Toyota/Scion iQ** is a recent exception that has been adapted for different markets. It is a compact city car first developed in 2007, sold in Japan and Europe from 2008, and available in the U.S. as a battery electric commuter car, mainly for short distance car-sharing projects in California.

Biofuel power

Various green renewable biofuels are being used as alternatives to gasoline and diesel and reduce vehicle emissions. Ethanol, made by fermenting sugar and starch crops, is being developed in the U.S. and Brazil. In Europe the most common biofuel is biodiesel, produced from fats and oils. The largest retailer in the U.S., Walmart, owns a fleet of delivery trucks converted to run on a biofuel made from reclaimed cooking grease produced during food preparation in its stores.

Solar energy

The World Solar Challenge is held every two years. From Darwin on the north coast of Australia to Adelaide on the south, specially designed solar cars, such as 2015's winning entry **Stella Lux**, are raced across 1,865 miles (3,000 km) of Australian outback. The technology developed for these solar cars could pave the way for new transportation options in the future, but so far there are no mass-produced solar cars.

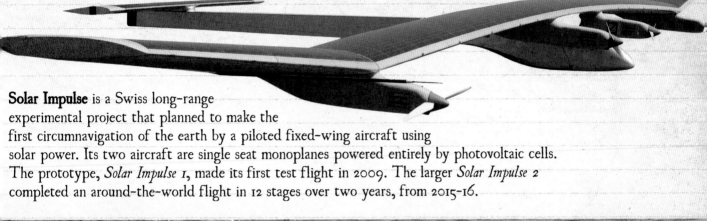

Solar Impulse is a Swiss long-range
experimental project that planned to make the
first circumnavigation of the earth by a piloted fixed-wing aircraft using
solar power. Its two aircraft are single seat monoplanes powered entirely by photovoltaic cells.
The prototype, *Solar Impulse 1*, made its first test flight in 2009. The larger *Solar Impulse 2*
completed an around-the-world flight in 12 stages over two years, from 2015-16.

This 102-ft (31 m) catamaran, called *Türanor
PlanetSolar*, is the largest solar-powered boat in the
world. It is covered in 5,780 sq ft (537 m²) of
solar panels and, by storing energy in batteries,
it is able to travel nonstop, day and night. In 2012,
it became the first solar-powered boat to
circumnavigate the globe. The journey took
one year, seven months and seven days.

Going electric
It's early days for electric motorbikes, which
are not yet made in large numbers. More will
be developed and costs will come down as
battery technology improves. At present their
range on fully charged batteries is less than
half the journey distance of a full tank of
gasoline, which can last up to 186m (300km).

IN THE AIR

For thousands of years, people watched the birds' mastery of the air and dreamed of joining them. The first people to fly used balloons that blew where the wind took them. Then, at the beginning of the 20th century, the Wright brothers learned the secret of powered flight. These early adventures led to today's air transportation industry and military air forces.

Look up into a clear blue sky and you may see a tiny speck streaking through the air. It is probably an airliner flying at almost 600 mph (1,000 km/h), 6 miles (10 km) above the Earth. It may not return to the ground for another 8,000 miles (13,000 km). There are more types of aircraft flying today than ever before — from hang-gliders and airships to airliners and supersonic research planes.

A **Boeing 787-8** is around 1,000 times heavier than the **Blériot XI monoplane**, which made the first airplane flight across the English Channel in 1909.

Saab 35 Draken fighter plane, first built in 1955

Blériot XI monoplane

What is a plane?

A typical plane has a long slender fuselage (body), with a wing on each side. The tail has a vertical fin and tailplane (horizontal stabilizer). There is an engine in its nose, or two or more engines attached to its wings or mounted on its tail. Wheels may fold up into the nose and wings after takeoff.

Biplane

Straight wing

The parts of a plane

This small plane is powered by two jet engines in its tail. The pilot steers by moving controls that tilt parts of the wings and tail. Ailerons in the wings make the plane roll, the rudder in the fin turns the nose right or left, and elevators in the tailplane tip the nose up or down. Flaps assist takeoff and landing.

Elevator

Tailplane

Fin

Rudder

Passenger area

Radio antenna

Aileron

Fuselage

Flaps

Nose cone with radar

LEARJET

Cockpit

Nose wheel

Wing struts

Main landing gear

Wing

Lift and flight

Planes fly because of the shape of their wings. Air flowing over the curved top speeds up and has a lower pressure than air passing underneath.

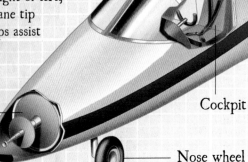

Low pressure

Lift

High pressure

Lift

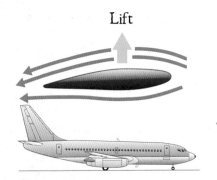

1. As a plane starts moving, its wings cut through the air and create lift.

Increased lift

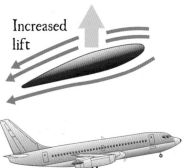

2. When its nose tips up and the wings tilt, they create even more lift.

Swept-back wing

Folding wing

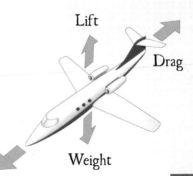

Delta wing

Types of wings

The slowest aircraft are biplanes and other straight-winged airplanes. Faster airliners have swept-back wings. Supersonic aircraft have triangular "delta" or diamond-shaped wings. Navy planes have folding wings to fit the most planes in the smallest space. Some planes have turned-up wingtips, or winglets, to reduce drag and save fuel.

The forces of flight

Four forces act on every airplane. Engine power thrusts it forward; air pushing back against it causes drag, trying to slow it down. Wings create lift, which acts upward, while its weight tries to pull it downward.

Lift

Drag

Weight

Thrust

Gossamer Penguin (right) was a solar-powered aircraft designed by Dr. Paul MacCready and initially flown by his son, who was 13 and weighed about 80 lb (36 kg). The plane itself only weighed 65 lb (30 kg)! The first test flight was in 1980. The first official flight flown by Janice Brown traveled just over 2 miles (3 km) in 14 minutes and 21 seconds and used solar power directly.

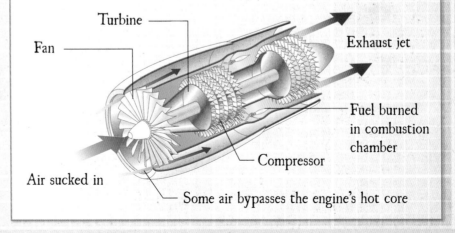

Jet engine

All but the smallest planes are powered by jet engines. These consist of several parts. A spinning fan at the front sucks in air. Some of this air is squashed in a compressor and is heated by burning fuel so that it expands and rushes out of the engine as a fast jet. The jet spins a windmill-like turbine, which drives the fan and compressor. The rest of the air flows around the engine's hot core.

Turbine

Fan

Exhaust jet

Fuel burned in combustion chamber

Compressor

Air sucked in

Some air bypasses the engine's hot core

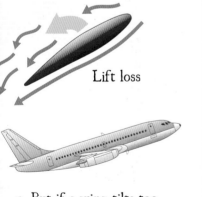

Lift loss

3. But if a wing tilts too much, the air above it breaks up and it loses lift.

The Wright brothers

Amerian brothers Wilbur and Orville Wright made the vital breakthrough in the search for a method of powered flight. They began by building a series of gliders, each improving on the one before. Then they designed the world's first successful powered airplane, the 1903 *Wright Flyer*. During this time they also designed and made their own engine and propellers. In 1908, Wilbur Wright took an improved version of the *Flyer* to France and dazzled Europeans with his displays of controlled flying.

In the air!

The world's first controlled, powered airplane flight took place on the morning of December 17, 1903, at Kill Devil Hills in North Carolina. At about 10:35 a.m., a small group of local spectators who had gathered saw Orville take off, fly into the wind for 12 seconds, and land 118 ft (36 m) away. Later the same day, Wilbur made another flight, which lasted 59 seconds and covered a distance of 850 ft (259 m).

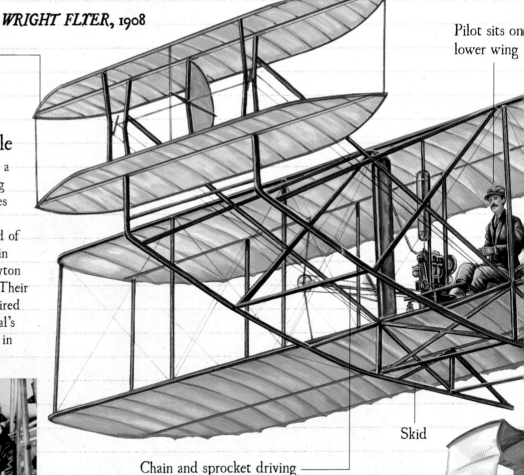

WRIGHT FLYER, 1908

Elevators

Pilot sits on lower wing

Skid

Chain and sprocket driving propeller from engine

Wilbur and Orville

The Wright brothers had a prosperous business selling and manufacturing bicycles in Dayton, Ohio. Wilbur was born in 1867 and died of typhoid fever in Dayton in 1912. Orville, born in Dayton in 1871, lived until 1948. Their interest in flight was inspired by news of Otto Lilienthal's glider flights in Germany in the 1890s.

The first airplane flight in Europe was not made until 1906. Alberto Santos-Dumont, a Brazilian living in France, made a series of short flights in his plane, 14-bis.

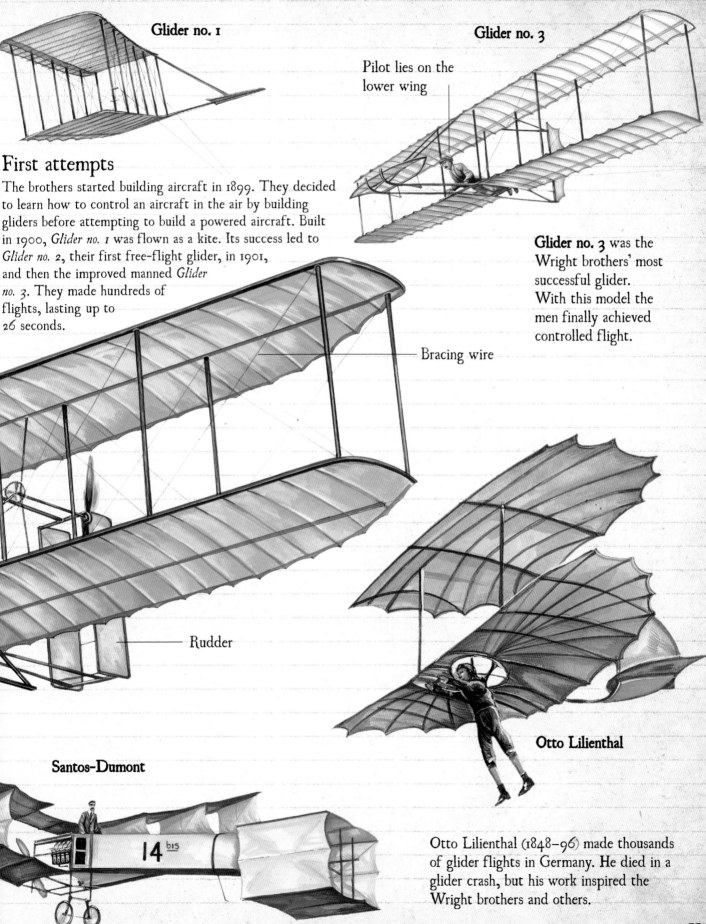

Glider no. 1

Glider no. 3

Pilot lies on the lower wing

First attempts

The brothers started building aircraft in 1899. They decided to learn how to control an aircraft in the air by building gliders before attempting to build a powered aircraft. Built in 1900, *Glider no. 1* was flown as a kite. Its success led to *Glider no. 2*, their first free-flight glider, in 1901, and then the improved manned *Glider no. 3*. They made hundreds of flights, lasting up to 26 seconds.

Glider no. 3 was the Wright brothers' most successful glider. With this model the men finally achieved controlled flight.

— Bracing wire

— Rudder

Otto Lilienthal

Santos-Dumont

14 bis

Otto Lilienthal (1848–96) made thousands of glider flights in Germany. He died in a glider crash, but his work inspired the Wright brothers and others.

Airforce airplanes

The first military planes were built during World War I (1914–18). They were flimsy craft — made from a wooden frame covered with fabric and powered by piston engines that drove the propellers. Their main task was to spot artillery. Fighters were built to stop the other side from doing such spying. Bombers were designed for attacking targets on the ground, and transport planes for carrying troops and supplies. Military planes today are simply bigger, heavier, all-metal and jet-engined versions of these early craft.

Sopwith Camel

Probably the greatest fighter aircraft of World War I, the Sopwith Camel could twist and turn tightly in air fights. But it could be difficult to control and inexperienced pilots often crashed while learning to fly it. Although known by everyone as the Sopwith Camel, it was actually called the Sopwith F1. "Camel" was a nickname that came from the hump over the twin machine guns on its nose.

Country: UK
Date: 1917
Size: 28-ft (8.5 m) wingspan
Construction: wood and fabric
Top speed: 105 mph (168 km/h)
On board: 1

Boeing B-17

More than 12,000 B-17s, or "Flying Fortresses," were built during World War II (1939–45). It was a long-range daylight heavy bomber. It could climb to over 33,000 ft (10,000 m) — as high as modern jet airliners — and its fuel tanks could take it 1,100 miles (1,700 km). The B-17 carried up to 6,000 lb (2,700 kg) of bombs, and was also armed with up to 13 machine guns to fight off attacks from enemy planes.

Country: U.S.
Date: 1935
Size: 104-ft (32 m) wingspan
Construction: armored alloy
Top speed: 287 mph (462 km/h)
On board: 10

North American Aviation P-51 Mustang

The P-51 Mustang was the best all-around fighter of World War II (1939–45). It was a combination of American air frame with a British Rolls-Royce Merlin engine. More than 15,000 Mustangs were built during the war. They were armed with six machine guns and carried up to 2,000 lb (900 kg) of bombs and extra fuel tanks.

Country: U.S.
Date: 1940
Size: 37-ft (11.3 m) wingspan
Construction: lightweight alloy
Top speed: 437 mph (703 km/h)
On board: 1

Boeing B-52 Stratofortress

A giant among bombers, the *B-52* is still in service. It can carry over 50,000 lb (22,700 kg) of bombs and missiles. It has a range of over 10,000 miles (16,000 km) — halfway around the world. Remote-controlled machine guns in its tail fight off attacks.

Country: U.S.
Date: 1952
Size: 185-ft (56 m) wingspan
Construction: armored alloy
Top speed: 595 mph (958 km/h)
On board: 6

F-15 Eagle

This is a long-range fighter that can also be used as a bomber and ground-attack aircraft. Its two side-by-side jet engines can power it to two and half times the speed of sound, and it can climb to 60,000 ft (18,000 m).

Country: UK
Date: 1966
Size: 30-ft (9 m) wingspan
Construction: lightweight alloy
Top speed: 660 mph (1,065 km/h)
On board: 1

British Aerospace Harrier Jet

The Harrier was the first VTOL (vertical takeoff and landing) combat plane. Its engine nozzles swivel so that the jets from the engine can be pointed downward for takeoff, and then can be swung backward for flying. It made its combat debut in the Falklands War (1982), where Harriers operated from aircraft carriers and the decks of cargo ships.

Country: U.S.
Date: 1972
Size: 42-ft (13 m) wingspan
Construction: lightweight alloy
Top speed: 1,675 mph (2,700 km/h)
On board: 2

Country: U.S.
Date: 1981
Size: 43-ft (13.5 m) wingspan
Construction: alloy and composites
Top speed: 645 mph (1,040 km/h)
On board: 1

Lockheed F-117 Nighthawk

Better known as the "Stealth Fighter," the F-117 attacks ground targets with pinpoint accuracy. It uses laser-guided bombs stored in its weapons bays. Its shape and black coating make it almost invisible on enemy radar.

Airliners

In the 1930s, the first propellered airliners flew their passengers slow and low, because piston engines were not very powerful. Flying boats also took wealthy people across continents. From the 1960s, jet airliners flew higher and faster, and were affordable for vacationers. The biggest airliner is the Boeing 747-400, which can carry 568 passengers. It is flown by a crew of only two, as computers have now replaced the flight engineer.

Country: U.S.
Date: 1933
Size: 74-ft (22.6 m) wingspan
Body: lightweight alloy
Top speed: 189 mph (304 km/h)
On board: 2 crew, 10 passengers

Boeing 247

The first modern airliner, the Boeing 247 was a streamlined all-metal plane. It had a retractable undercarriage — wheels that folded up inside it. It was safe and reliable because it could climb and cruise using only one of its two engines. It was designed as a mail-carrying plane, with only 10 seats for passengers.

Country: U.S.
Date: 1943
Size: 123-ft (37.5 m) wingspan
Construction: lightweight alloy
Top speed: 339 mph (545 km/h)
On board: 4 crew, 81 passengers

Lockheed Constellation

Although designed as a long-range airliner, the first Lockheed Constellations came off the assembly line during World War II (1939–45), so they entered service as a military transport plane. This plane's elegant, slender shape and comfortable, pressurized passenger cabin made it popular with airlines and passengers. Larger versions followed in the 1950s.

Country: UK
Date: 1949
Size: 115-ft (35 m) wingspan
Construction: lightweight alloy
Top speed: 490 mph (790 km/h)
On board: 3 crew, 44 passengers

Douglas DC-3

This airliner looks surprisingly modern for an airplane that made its first flight in 1935. More than 13,000 DC-3s were built. It was so successful that by 1938 most American air travelers flew in DC-3s. It served as a transporter during World War II and returned to airline service after the war. Remarkably, in 1999 about 200 DC-3s were still in civil and military service.

Country: U.S.
Date: 1935
Size: 95-ft (29 m) wingspan
Construction: lightweight alloy
Top speed: 185 mph (298 km/h)
On board: 2 crew, 21 passengers

De Havilland Comet

The Comet was the world's first jet airliner. Passengers loved it because it flew higher and faster than any other airliner. However, it suffered a weakness in its metal skin that allowed it to crack. It was completely re-designed and flew again on transatlantic routes as the larger Comet 4. But by then Boeing's bigger and faster 707 was flying.

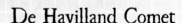

Boeing 747-100

The 747 "Jumbo Jet" began as a design for a military transporter, which Boeing changed into an airliner. Powered by four turbofan engines, it was the biggest airliner and the first of a new type, called a wide-bodied jet. The 747's passenger cabin had an upper deck and a first-class lounge.

Country: U.S.
Date: 1969
Size: 196-ft (59.6 m) wingspan
Construction: lightweight alloy
Top speed: 640 mph (1,030 km/h)
On board: 3 crew, 490 passengers

BAC/Aerospatiale Concorde

Concorde was the first supersonic airliner, able to fly at Mach 2 (twice the speed of sound) and cruising at 60,000 ft (18,000 m), where the sky above is black, like space. It could fly from London to New York in just three and a half hours, less than half the normal flight time. Concorde was developed as a joint project between Britain and France. Although it was a technological triumph, this was a very expensive project that only benefited a tiny number of wealthy passengers. British Airways and Air France both closed down their Concorde services in 2003, claiming they were no longer economically viable. It is unlikely that supersonic air travel will be revived.

Country: UK, France
Date: 1969
Size: 84-ft (25.6 m) wingspan
Construction: lightweight alloy
Top speed: 1,450 mph (2,333 km/h)
On board: 3 crew, 144 passengers

Country: Europe
Date: 2007
Size: 261.6-ft (79.75 m) wingspan
Construction: lightweight alloy
Top speed: 677 mph (1090 km/h)
On board: 2 crew, typically 544 passengers, up to 853.

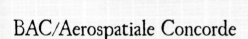

Airbus 380

The A380 is the latest and largest in the series of European Airbus airliners that started with the A300 in 1972. The four-engine jet is the biggest passenger airliner in the world and weighs up to 635 tons (575 tonnes) on takeoff. It also has the longest range of all the Airbuses, capable of traveling 9,450 miles (15,200 km) in a single flight. It has seating on two decks, and its most luxurious first-class seats can be fully reclined into beds.

Light aircraft

Light aircraft are small planes with many uses, such as pilot training, crop spraying and aerial photography. They are also used for "flying doctors." Most are flown for business and pleasure. A great deal of leisure flying is done in gliders, soaring into the sky on rising air currents. Hang gliders, where the pilot hangs underneath a kitelike wing, also use these rising "thermals" to stay airborne. Microlights are for one or two people: a three-axis microlight is steered by a control stick and pedals like larger aircraft, while a flexwing is steered by moving a bar attached to the wing.

Blériot Type XI

On July 25, 1909, Frenchman Louis Blériot flew his monoplane 24$\frac{1}{2}$ miles (39.4 km) across the English Channel — from Calais to Dover. This first cross-Channel flight took just 36 minutes. His single-wing, separate-tail, engine in-front design set the standard for air transportation. Over 100 XIs were ordered.

Country: France
Date: 1909
Size: 25-ft (7.8 m) wingspan
Construction: wood with stretched fabric
Top speed: 36 mph (58 km/h)
On board: 1 pilot

Cessna 172

The Cessna 170 series is the most successful light aircraft. The first 170 flew in 1948, the 172 flew seven years later. These aircraft were used for business and leisure flying, and for training pilots. Many improvements were made with more powerful engines and retractable (folding) landing gear. In 1958, a 172 was flown for 64 days nonstop. Food and fuel were hoisted up from a truck racing down an airport runway!

Country: U.S.
Date: 1955
Size: 35 ¾-ft (10.9 m) wingspan
Construction: lightweight alloy
Top speed: 140 mph (226 km/h)
On board: 1 pilot, 3 passengers

Piper PA-28 Cherokee

The Piper PA-28 Cherokee was built to compete with the popular Cessna 172, which it did very successfully. It was used for pilot training, leisure flying and touring all over the world. Piper brought out new models with more powerful engines and better control.

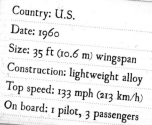

Country: U.S.
Date: 1960
Size: 35 ft (10.6 m) wingspan
Construction: lightweight alloy
Top speed: 133 mph (213 km/h)
On board: 1 pilot, 3 passengers

Learjet

The Learjet is the classic business jet. It was named after William P. Lear, who developed the design. The first Learjet was an instant success because of its good looks, reasonable price and high speed. Because of its small size, light weight and the power of its twin jet engines, it could climb faster than a fighter. Further versions were built, increasing its range from 1,584 miles (2,549 km) to 3,155 miles (5,078 km) and its passenger-carrying capacity from five to nine.

Country: U.S.
Date: 1963
Size: 35½-ft (10.8 m) wingspan
Construction: lightweight alloy
Top speed: 549 mph (884 km/h)
On board: 2 crew, 5 passengers

Country: UK
Date: 1993
Size: 30¾-ft (9.4 m) wingspan
Construction: composite frame
Top speed: 50 mph (80 km/h)
On board: 1 pilot

Country: Germany
Date: 1993
Size: 65½-ft (20 m) wingspan
Construction: fiberglass
Top speed: 155 mph (250 km/h)
On board: 2

Duo Discus Glider

From 1985 to 1995 the Discus won six world gliding championships. To save weight, its slender body and swept-back wings are made from fiberglass and foam plastic. The slightly larger two-seater Duo model is based on this successful single-seater, and is used for training.

Pegasus Breeze

This hang glider was first developed from a kitelike wing as a NASA project designed by Dr. Francis Rogallo to land U.S. spacecraft back on Earth. However, it was never used for that, and instead, was developed for the new sport of hang gliding. Weighing only 61½ lb (28 kg), it has a semi-rigid wing with material stretched over a frame.

Flexwing Microlight

The Quantum 912 Flexwing is a weight-shift microlight, steered by moving a bar attached to the wing. It can carry a pilot and passenger with a combined weight of up to 375 lb (172 kg). Fully loaded, it can climb at 1,200 ft (365 m) per minute.

Country: UK
Date: 1995
Size: 34-ft (10.35 m) wingspan
Construction: alloy and composites
Top speed: 88 mph (140 km/h)
On board: 1 to 2

Helicopters

The first helicopter flight was in 1907. It took another 30 years to develop the first practical helicopter, the Vought-Sikorsky VS-300, because of formidable technical problems. Once these were solved, helicopters progressed rapidly. Until the 1950s, the rotors (blades) of early helicopters were powered by piston engines. Then more powerful turboshaft ("jet"-type) engines became available. From air-sea rescue to police surveillance, helicopters are highly versatile machines.

Country: U.S.
Date: 1942
Size: 38-ft (11.6 m) rotors
Construction: fabric and aluminum alloy
Top speed: 81 mph (131 km/h)
On board: 1 crew, 1 passenger

Sikorsky R-4

Sikorsky transformed his experimental VS-300 (see below) into a production model, the R-4, by covering it with fabric and giving it an enclosed cockpit. Its simple layout and easy maintenance made it a popular military helicopter.

Breguet-Richet No. 1

On September 29, 1907, at Douai in France, the Breguet-Richet No. 1 became the first man-carrying helicopter to leave the ground. The lift was created by four rotors driven by a 50 horsepower Antoinette engine. The ungainly craft was very unstable and had to be steadied by four men with poles.

Country: France
Date: 1907
Size: four 26¼-ft (8 m) rotors
Construction: wood and metal frame
Top speed: zero (hovered only)
On board: 1 crew

Country: U.S.
Date: 1961
Size: 60-ft (18.3 m) rotors
Construction: aluminum alloy
Top speed: 160 mph (256 km/h)
On board: 2 crew, 55 passengers

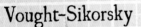

Vought-Sikorsky

The modern helicopter, with a large overhead rotor and small tail rotor to balance the twisting effect of the main rotor, was developed in the 1930s by Igor Sikorsky. His VS-300 lifted off for the first time on September 14, 1939 and made its first untethered flight on May 13, 1940.

Country: U.S.
Date: 1939
Size: 38-ft (11.6 m) rotors
Construction: tubular metal frame
Top speed: unknown
On board: 1 crew

CH-47 Chinook

The Chinook was developed to meet the U.S. Army's need for an all-weather transport helicopter. The current model, the CH-47D, can carry 55 troops and 11 tons (10 tonnes) of cargo slung underneath it or 6.6 tons (6 tonnes) inside.

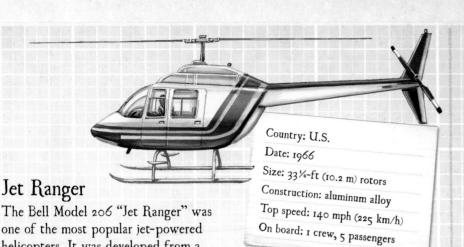

Hughes AH-64 Apache

The American Apache is a formidable fighting machine. It was developed in the 1980s to attack armored vehicles. It can operate day or night, and in all weathers. Advanced sensors enable it to find targets and lock its missiles onto them.

Jet Ranger

The Bell Model 206 "Jet Ranger" was one of the most popular jet-powered helicopters. It was developed from a military helicopter, the Bell OH-4A, with a range of 388 miles (624 km). By 1977, 5,000 military and civil models had been built.

Country: U.S.
Date: 1966
Size: 33¼-ft (10.2 m) rotors
Construction: aluminum alloy
Top speed: 140 mph (225 km/h)
On board: 1 crew, 5 passengers

Country: U.S.
Date: 1982
Size: 48-ft (14.6 m) rotors
Construction: armored aluminum alloy
Top speed: 187 mph (300 km/h)
On board: 2 crew

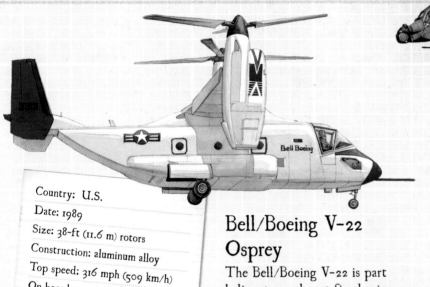

Country: U.S.
Date: 1989
Size: 38-ft (11.6 m) rotors
Construction: aluminum alloy
Top speed: 316 mph (509 km/h)
On board: 2 crew, 24 passengers

Bell/Boeing V-22 Osprey

The Bell/Boeing V-22 is part helicopter and part fixed-wing aircraft. It takes off vertically like a helicopter. Then its engines swing forward so that the rotors become propellers. This enables the V-22 to fly faster than any helicopter.

Mil Mi-24 Hind

The Mil Mi-24 Hind was the first Russian purpose-built attack helicopter. It is used as an anti-tank "gunship" and also for transporting up to 12 troops. The two cockpits in the nose are heavily armored to protect the crew from ground fire.

Country: Russia
Date: 1970
Size: 56¾-ft (17.3 m) rotors
Construction: armored aluminum alloy
Top speed: 190 mph (310 km/h)
On board: 2 crew, 12 passengers

Balloons and airships

The first people to fly were carried aloft by nothing more than a balloon, which floated upward because hot air and hydrogen gas are lighter than the surrounding cold air. Balloons would drift wherever the wind blew them, but by fitting an engine and propeller, steering was possible, and the balloon became a sausage-shaped airship or dirigible. Modern airships are filled with non-flammable helium gas.

Country: France
Date: 1783
Size: 49 ft (15 m) across
Construction: fabric
Top speed: 12½ mph (20 km/h)
On board: 2

Montgolfier balloon

Two French brothers, Joseph Michel and Jacques Etienne Montgolfier, made the first manned flight on November 21, 1783. The air in the balloon was heated by a fire of straw. The craft drifted 5½ miles (8 km) across Paris in 25 minutes, and climbed to 1,500 ft (450 m).

Giffard airship

The first person to build an aircraft that could be steered (instead of drifting with the wind) was Henri Giffard. He hung a steam engine and propeller underneath a long, thin hydrogen-filled balloon, so that the spinning propeller pushed the craft through the air. In 1852, he flew his airship 17 miles (27 km) from Paris to Trappes.

Country: France
Date: 1852
Size: 144 ft (43.9 m) long
Construction: fabric
Top speed: 5 mph (8 km/h)
On board: 1

Nulli Secundus

The British Army's first airship was completed in 1907. It was called Dirigible number 1, better known as *Nulli Secundus*, meaning "second to none." It was built by U.S.-born British aviator Samuel Franklin Cody.

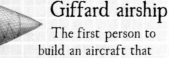

Country: UK
Date: 1907
Size: 122 ft (37 m) long
Construction: animal skin
Top speed: 20 mph (32 km/h)
On board: 2

ZR-1 Shenandoah

The U.S. Navy's first rigid airship was made from a lightweight metal frame with fabric stretched over it. It was also the first to be filled with helium gas instead of hydrogen, and it carried 50,000 lb (22,000 kg) of fuel and cargo.

Country: U.S.
Date: 1923
Size: 680 ft (207 m) long
Construction: fabric over alloy frame
Top speed: 81 mph (130 km/h)
On board: 43 (on last flight)

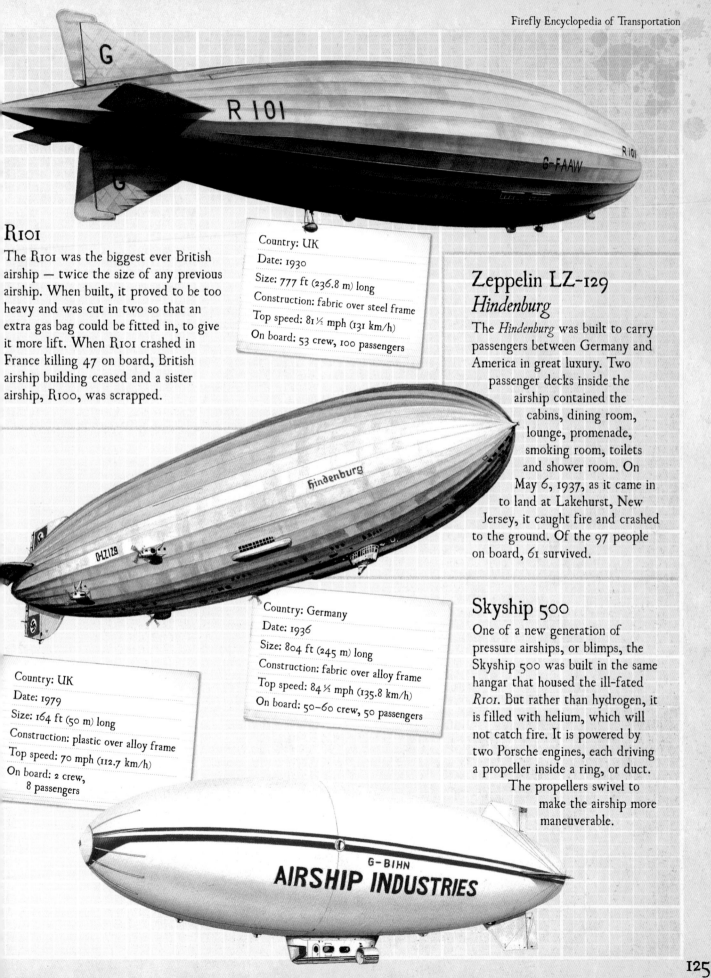

R101

The R101 was the biggest ever British airship — twice the size of any previous airship. When built, it proved to be too heavy and was cut in two so that an extra gas bag could be fitted in, to give it more lift. When R101 crashed in France killing 47 on board, British airship building ceased and a sister airship, R100, was scrapped.

Country: UK
Date: 1930
Size: 777 ft (236.8 m) long
Construction: fabric over steel frame
Top speed: 81½ mph (131 km/h)
On board: 53 crew, 100 passengers

Zeppelin LZ-129
Hindenburg

The *Hindenburg* was built to carry passengers between Germany and America in great luxury. Two passenger decks inside the airship contained the cabins, dining room, lounge, promenade, smoking room, toilets and shower room. On May 6, 1937, as it came in to land at Lakehurst, New Jersey, it caught fire and crashed to the ground. Of the 97 people on board, 61 survived.

Country: Germany
Date: 1936
Size: 804 ft (245 m) long
Construction: fabric over alloy frame
Top speed: 84½ mph (135.8 km/h)
On board: 50–60 crew, 50 passengers

Skyship 500

One of a new generation of pressure airships, or blimps, the Skyship 500 was built in the same hangar that housed the ill-fated *R101*. But rather than hydrogen, it is filled with helium, which will not catch fire. It is powered by two Porsche engines, each driving a propeller inside a ring, or duct. The propellers swivel to make the airship more maneuverable.

Country: UK
Date: 1979
Size: 164 ft (50 m) long
Construction: plastic over alloy frame
Top speed: 70 mph (112.7 km/h)
On board: 2 crew, 8 passengers

Around-the-world balloons

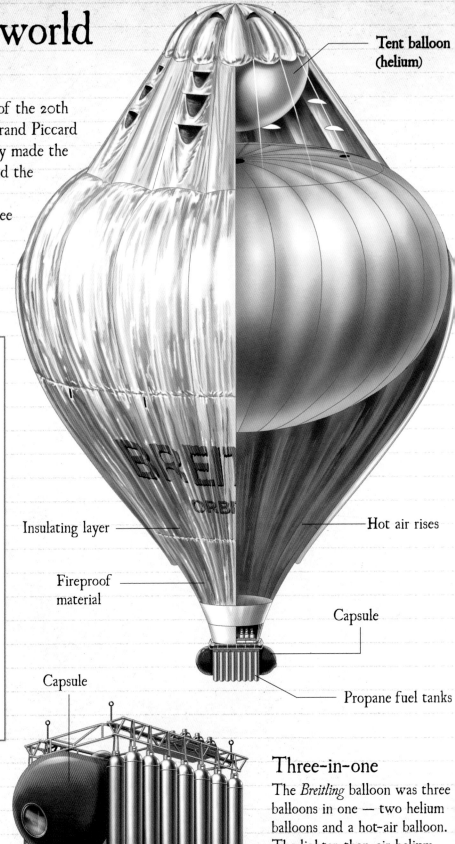

The last great aviation record of the 20th century was claimed by Bertrand Piccard and Brian Jones in 1999 when they made the first non-stop balloon flight around the world. Their historic flight in the *Breitling Orbiter 3* balloon took three weeks and covered a distance of 28,400 miles (45,700 km) at speeds of up to 115 mph (185 km/h).

Tent balloon (helium)

Insulating layer

Hot air rises

Fireproof material

Capsule

Propane fuel tanks

In the jet stream

If a balloon climbs higher than 32,800 ft (10,000 m), it enters a high-speed wind called the jet stream. Air speeds here can be extremely fast.

In the capsule

Breitling Orbiter 3 was designed to fly at up to 40,000 ft (12,200 m) above the ground. At that height, the air is too thin to breathe, so the crew flew inside a sealed capsule with its own air supply.

Capsule

Propane fuel tanks

Three-in-one

The *Breitling* balloon was three balloons in one — two helium balloons and a hot-air balloon. The lighter-than-air helium gas reduced the amount of fuel needed for the balloon's gas burners.

Orbiter's route

Breitling Orbiter 3 took off from Chàteau-d'Oex, Switzerland, on March 1, 1999. It drifted southwest before finding eastward winds over north Africa. Its route took it over the Middle East, India and China, then out across the Pacific Ocean. It crossed Mexico and set out over the Atlantic Ocean. On March 20, it crossed the finish line and landed in Egypt the next day.

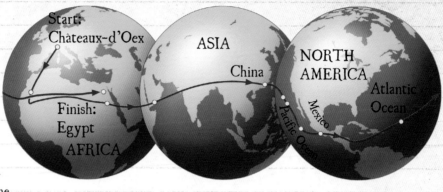

Piccard Balloon

Designed by Swiss physicist Auguste Piccard, this was the first "teardrop" shaped balloon designed to accommodate the expanding gas that helped it rise. It also featured the first sealed cabin. In May 1931, it became the first balloon to ascend into the stratosphere. Piccard, with Paul Kipfer on board, reached a height of 50,135 ft (15,281 m).

ICO Global Challenger

In December 1998, *ICO Global Challenger* carried Richard Branson, Per Lindstrand and Steve Fossett 12,404 miles (19,960 km) before they had to ditch in the Pacific Ocean near Hawaii.

Solo Spirit 3

Solo Spirit 3, piloted by Steve Fossett, plunged into the Coral Sea on August 16, 1998, when the balloon was torn apart by a thunderstorm. It had flown 14,236 miles (22,900 km). Fossett was rescued from the sea the next day.

Traffic watch

In ancient times, when there were few carts on the road or ships on the oceans, traffic looked after itself. The first traffic lights were used in Cleveland, Ohio, in 1914. Today, our heavy traffic needs even more controlling, to keep it safe and to help it run smoothly. The simple hand signals of a policeman, or a set of colored traffic lights, are still much in use to keep the roads free of congestion. However, there are also much more modern traffic systems based on computers, satellites and radar systems to prevent air, sea and train accidents.

Air traffic controllers guide aircraft especially during takeoff and landing and through congested air space. They use radar to keep aircraft on precise routes called airways that ensure they are a safe distance from each other, and to bring them safely in to land.

Stacking is a way of dealing with aircraft as they wait to come in to land. The waiting airplanes fly in a series of ovals. Each aircraft sticks to a different altitude so that they are all kept safely apart. As the first plane lands, the others move down the stack.

Coming in to land, pilots leave the holding stack (if they are not coming in to land directly) and follow a route called a glide path, on which radio signals guide the planes safely down toward the runway. Once on the ground, the pilots steer their aircraft to one of the taxiways, clearing the runway for the next takeoff or landing.

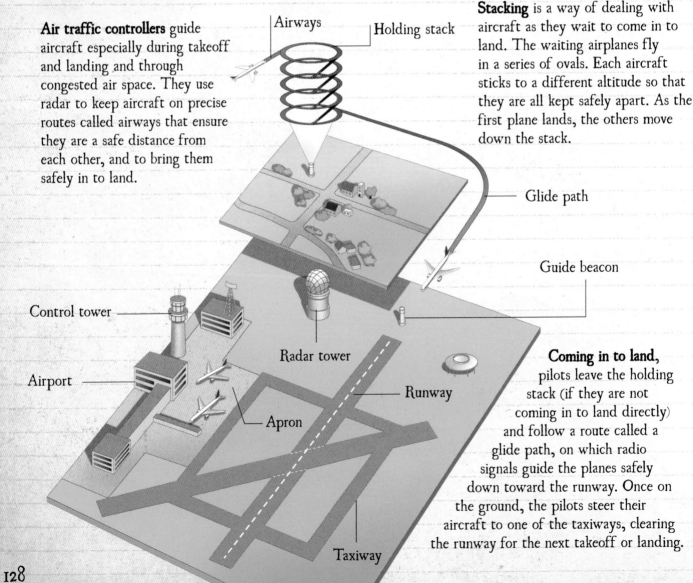

Airways

Holding stack

Glide path

Guide beacon

Control tower

Radar tower

Airport

Runway

Apron

Taxiway

Traffic signals may be computer controlled, with sensors to assess the traffic flow and switch the lights to keep vehicles moving. Many traffic lights also have a button for pedestrians to press to cross the road.

Traffic police can respond quickly to any situation, dealing with traffic jams and accidents, and re-routing cars in emergencies.

Tolls are used on many highways and bridges to pay for the upkeep of those routes. Vehicles stop at a booth where drivers pay to use the road, or cars are photographed or electronically monitored as they travel the toll road, and billed. Traffic can also be counted and monitored through tolls.

Railway signal operators use computers to control whole lengths of track and to display each train's position. Signals can be set so drivers will stop if they get too close to another train.

At **level crossings,** roads pass over railway tracks. Signal lights and barriers tell road users when to stop for passing trains.

IN SPACE

In 1961, Soviet pilot Yuri Gagarin rocketed out of the atmosphere in his Vostok capsule and orbited the Earth. His historic flight marked the beginning of manned space flight. Since then, unmanned spacecraft have explored the solar system and people have lived in space stations and landed on the Moon. Now, space shuttles ferry people into Earth's orbit and back.

Space flight is the youngest of all the different forms of transportation, so it is not available to all of us — yet. But, just as airplanes were once flown only by a small group of intrepid pioneers and now carry millions of passengers each year, "space planes" may one day be an equally popular transportation.

When orbiting the Earth, the **Hubble Space Telescope** is able to give astronomers sharper photographs of the stars and galaxies than is possible from the Earth's surface. This is because the Earth's atmosphere distorts images of space.

Salyut 1 space station

The Space Shuttle orbiting Earth

What is a spacecraft?

Spacecraft are vehicles designed to travel in space. They include satellites orbiting the Earth, probes sent to the planets, and manned vehicles such as the American space shuttle and Russian *Soyuz* craft. They are launched by immensely powerful rockets. In space, they steer by firing smaller thrusters.

Robert H. Goddard, an American scientist, launched the first liquid-fuel rocket at Auburn, Massachusetts, on March 16, 1926. It flew 184 ft (56 m) in 2.5 seconds.

The German V-2 was the first successful modern rocket. It stood 56 ft (14 m) high and weighed 27,500 lb (12,500 kg).

Alcohol fuel tank

Liquid oxygen tank

V-2 rocket

German scientists and engineers developed the V-2 rocket weapon during World War II (1939–45). It carried a 2,200-lb (1,000-kg) warhead a distance of 171 miles (275 km), faster than the speed of sound.

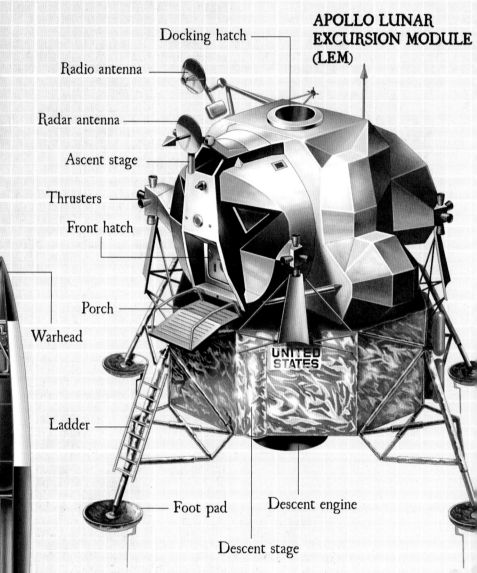

APOLLO LUNAR EXCURSION MODULE (LEM)

Docking hatch

Radio antenna

Radar antenna

Ascent stage

Thrusters

Front hatch

Porch

Ladder

Warhead

Foot pad

Descent engine

Descent stage

UNITED STATES

Spacecraft anatomy

The Apollo Lunar Excursion Module (LEM) could land two astronauts on the Moon. It was a very unusual spacecraft. The base, or descent stage, had a rocket engine to slow down the LEM for landing. Then, at the end of the mission, the LEM split in two and the descent stage formed a launch pad for the upper part, or ascent stage. It steered by firing thrusters arranged in groups of four. Broad foot pads ensured that it did not sink into the Moon's surface.

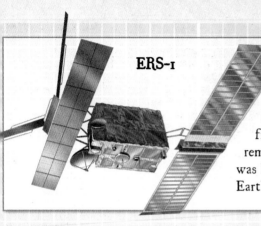

ERS-1

Remote sensing

Remote sensing satellites collect information about the Earth or another planet from space. The European remote sensing satellite (ERS-1) was launched in 1991 to study the Earth, its oceans and atmosphere.

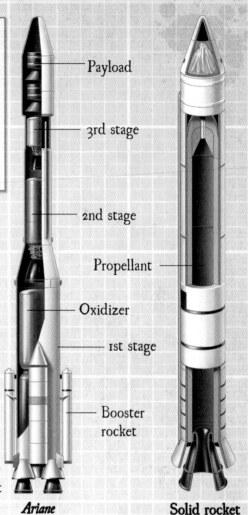

- Payload
- 3rd stage
- 2nd stage
- Propellant
- Oxidizer
- 1st stage
- Booster rocket

Ariane

Solid rocket booster

Spacecraft

All spacecraft need electricity to power their instruments and communications equipment. Most spacecraft make electricity from sunlight by using solar panels. Beyond the orbit of Mars, there is too little sunlight for solar panels to work, so space probes going to the outer planets use nuclear generators. American manned spacecraft use fuel cells to make electricity from a chemical reaction between hydrogen and oxygen.

Rocket types

Rockets, such as the European *Ariane* launcher, burn liquid fuel. *Ariane*'s liquid engines are assisted by two strap-on solid propellant engines. Burning requires oxygen, so the fuel is mixed with a liquid called an oxidizer that provides the oxygen. Liquid fuel rocket engines are controllable. They can be turned on and off, and varied in power, by pumping more or less fuel into the engine. Another type of rocket burns solid propellant, a mixture of solid fuel and oxidizer. Once lit, it burns until no propellant is left.

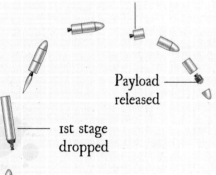

2nd stage dropped

Payload released

1st stage dropped

Rocket launch

A rocket is actually several rockets, called stages, stacked on top of each other. Each stage falls away as it runs out of fuel.

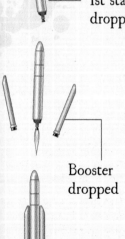

Booster dropped

Lift off

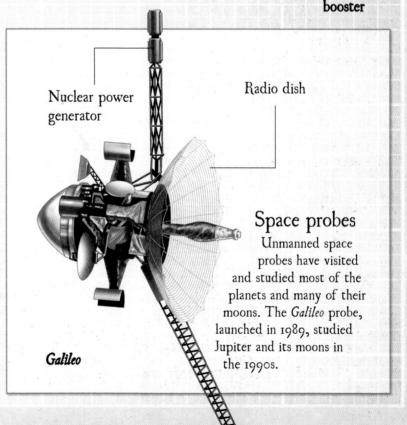

Nuclear power generator

Radio dish

Galileo

Space probes

Unmanned space probes have visited and studied most of the planets and many of their moons. The *Galileo* probe, launched in 1989, studied Jupiter and its moons in the 1990s.

Satellites and probes

The Space Age began on October 4, 1957, when Russia sent the first man-made object into orbit. It was called *Sputnik*, meaning "traveler." Other unmanned spacecraft were launched to explore the solar system. They landed on the Moon, photographed the planets, mapped Venus and looked for life on Mars. Today, some satellites orbit the Earth to monitor the weather. Others study the universe with telescopes. Probes have visited Jupiter and the outer planets, acting as the robot eyes and ears of scientists and astronauts who may follow them one day.

Country: Russia
Date: 1957
Size: 2 ft (58 cm) across
Construction: metal sphere
Top speed: 17,500 mph (28,000 km/h)

Sputnik-1

A metal ball with a radio transmitter, *Sputnik-1* had four long antennae to send its bleeps to an amazed world. Its launch sparked a "space race" between the U.S. and Russia that lasted until Apollo 11 in 1969.

Surveyor 3

Landing on a part of the Moon called the Ocean of Storms, *Surveyor 3* took 6,315 photographs of the Moon's surface. It dug a small trench in the ground to test the Moon's strength in preparation for later manned landings. In 1969, Apollo 12 landed near the craft and astronauts brought parts of the *Surveyor* back to Earth.

Country: U.S.
Date: 1967
Size: 10 ft (3 m) high
Construction: lightweight alloys
Top speed: 24,230 mph (39,000 km/h)

Viking

In 1976, two Viking spacecraft went into orbit around the planet Mars. They dropped probes onto the surface. The landers carried a chemical laboratory, a weather station that sent daily reports until 1983, and an instrument to study Mars-quakes. They took thousands of photographs, and also tested samples of the rust-red soil for signs of life on Mars. No life forms were detected.

Country: U.S.
Date: 1976
Size: 9¾ ft (3 m)
Construction: lightweight alloys
Top speed: 24,230 mph (39,000 km/h)

Voyager

The first close-up images and measurements of distant planets were taken by *Voyager*. New moons and rings around Jupiter were revealed. The instruments ran on nuclear power, and a radio dish 12 ft (3.7 m) across kept the probe in contact with Earth.

Country: U.S.

Date: 1977

Size: 9 ¾ ft (3 m) high

Construction: aluminum

Top speed: 32,000 mph (52,000 km/h)

Country: U.S.

Date: 1989

Size: 17 ½ ft (5.3 m) high

Construction: lightweight alloys

Top speed: 54,225 mph (86,760 km/h)

Galileo

In 1995, *Galileo* became the first spacecraft to orbit Jupiter. It was named after the great Italian scientist, Galileo Galilei, who discovered four of Jupiter's moons. A small probe was dropped into Jupiter's atmosphere. This sent back measurements for 57 minutes until it was destroyed by heat and crushing pressure.

Hubble Space Telescope

This orbiting telescope has given astronomers amazing pictures of stars forming and exploding with no interference from the Earth's atmosphere. But the first images were blurred because a mistake had been made when making the telescope's main mirror. Space shuttle astronauts repaired the telescope using the Canadarm.

Country: U.S.

Date: 1990

Size: 43 ½ ft (13.3 m) long

Construction: lightweight alloys

Top speed: 17,500 mph (28,000 km/h)

Cassini-Huygens

The largest space probe ever launched, *Cassini-Huygens* is two space probes in one. The main craft, *Cassini*, has studied the ringed planet Saturn since it arrived there in 2004. It carried a smaller probe, *Huygens*, which it dropped onto Saturn's largest moon, Titan in 2005. *Huygens* survived the landing and successfully sent data about its environment back to Earth.

Country: U.S., Europe

Date: 1997

Size: 22 ¼ ft (6.8 m) high

Construction: lightweight alloys

Top speed: 42,511 mph (68,400 km/h)

Taking man to the Moon

A new age in exploration and transportation began when Russian cosmonaut Yuri Gagarin became the first person to be launched into space. He made one orbit in his tiny capsule and returned safely to Earth. Not to be outdone, America launched its own series of manned spaceflights to learn how to control spacecraft and link them together. The "space race" was on and was "won" by the *Apollo* spacecraft landing 12 astronauts on the Moon between 1969 and 1972.

Mercury Redstone 3

The first American astronaut in space was Alan Shepard on board *Mercury Redstone 3 (MR-3)*. A *Redstone* rocket boosted his capsule *Freedom 7* to a height of 116 ½ miles (187.5 km). There was not enough power to place the capsule in orbit, so it re-entered the atmosphere and fell back to Earth.

Country: U.S.

Date: 1961

Size: 9 ½ ft (2.9 m)

Construction: lightweight alloys

Top speed: 5,180 mph (8,336 km/h)

On board: 1

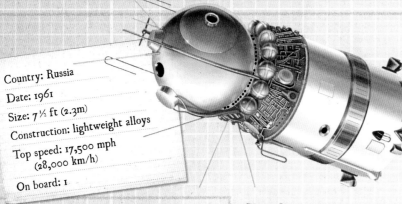

Country: Russia

Date: 1961

Size: 7 ½ ft (2.3m)

Construction: lightweight alloys

Top speed: 17,500 mph (28,000 km/h)

On board: 1

Mercury Atlas MA-6

John Glenn was the first American astronaut to orbit the Earth. His *Mercury* capsule, *Friendship 7*, was launched by an *Atlas* rocket (more powerful than the *Redstone* rockets on the early *Mercury* flights). After three orbits, when it seemed that the capsule's heat shield had come loose, Glenn's flight was cut short for fear it would burn up on re-entering the atmosphere. But Glenn landed safely.

Country: U.S.

Date: 1962

Size: 9 ½ ft (2.9 m)

Construction: lightweight alloys

Top speed: 17,543 mph (28,234 km/h)

On board: 1

Vostok 1

The *Vostok* (meaning "east" in Russian) *1* space capsule was a hollow metal ball just big enough for Yuri Gagarin to lie down inside for the flight lasting 1 hour 48 minutes. It was completely covered with heat shield material to protect him from the intense heat of re-entering the atmosphere. A rocket engine on the capsule was fired after one orbit to slow the capsule and make it fall back to Earth.

Gemini 6

Twice the size and weight of *Mercury*, the *Gemini* spacecraft carried a two-man crew. There were 10 *Gemini* flights in less than two years. *Gemini 6* was to be launched to maneuver close to a rocket already in space. But the rocket was lost, and *Gemini 6* was delayed a few months so that it could use *Gemini 7* as its target instead. *Gemini 6*, flown by Wally Schirra and Thomas Stafford, came within ¾ ft (0.3 m) of *Gemini 7*.

Country: U.S.

Date: 1965

Size: 18 ½ ft (5.6 m)

Body: lightweight alloys

Top speed: 17,500 mph (28,000 km/h)

On board: 2

Apollo 11

The *Saturn V* rocket powered the first astronauts to the Moon. The crew (Neil Armstrong, Edwin "Buzz" Aldrin and Michael Collins) lived in the tiny cone-shaped Command Module (CM) for the three-day flight to the Moon and the return journey. The Lunar Excursion Module (LEM) landed Armstrong and Aldrin on the surface.

Country: U.S.

Date: 1969

Size: CM 11½ ft (3.5 m); LEM 22¾ ft (7.0 m)

Construction: lightweight alloys

Top speed: 24,230 mph (39,000 km/h)

On board: 3

Soyuz 9

All *Soyuz* (meaning "union" in Russian) spacecraft have three parts. At one end, the instrument module contains radio equipment and rocket engines. Solar panels attached to it turn sunlight into electricity. The crew cannot get inside this module. In the middle is the descent module for getting back to Earth. At the other end, the crew work in the orbital module. *Soyuz 9* made a record-breaking 18-day flight.

Country: Russia

Date: 1970

Size: 23 ft (6.98 m)

Construction: lightweight alloys

Top speed: 17,500 mph (28,000 km/h)

On board: 2 to 3

Apollo–Soyuz project

A Russian *Soyuz* spacecraft and an American *Apollo* spacecraft docked with each other in orbit on the first joint space mission. The crews shared two days of scientific experiments. A disaster was narrowly avoided during the *Apollo* splashdown. The crew was almost poisoned by gas from the spacecraft control system.

Country: U.S., Russia

Date: 1975

Size: 68 ft (20.73 m) docked

Construction: lightweight alloys

Top speed: 17,500 mph (28,000 km/h)

On board: 5

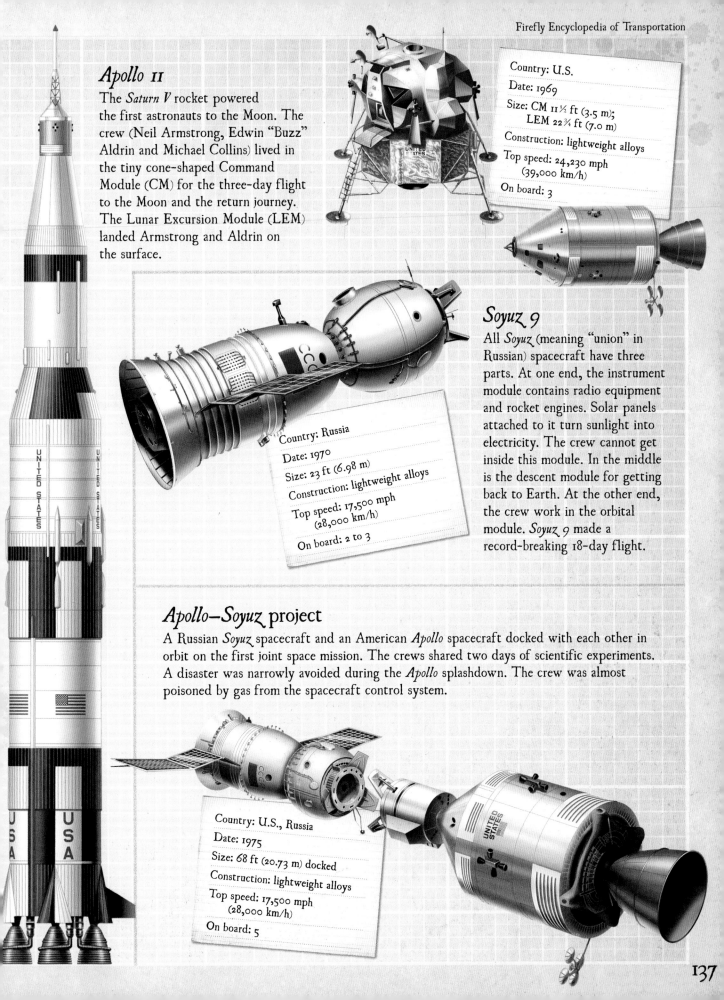

The space shuttle

The space shuttle was the first reusable spacecraft, developed by NASA in the 1970s. The three surviving craft were retired in 2012 after 30 years' service. A shuttle blasted off vertically like a rocket but could land again like an airliner on a runway. Within 14 days, it could b made ready for another flight. Its main job was to carry satellites, experiments, and parts for the international space station into orbit. The immense thrust needed to launch the winged craft, called the orbiter, w supplied by three main engines in its tail, fed with fuel from an external tank and two solid rocket boosters.

A space shuttle launch was a spectacular sight. As space shuttle *Endeavour* took off (above), searing hot gases at 5,400 °F (3,000 °C) raced out of the orbiter's engines and its rocket boosters at 620 mph (10,000 km/h).

3.

2.

The orbiter

The orbiter was the space-plane of the space shuttle: it was 120 ft (37 m) long with a wingspan of 79 ft (24 m) — about the same size as a small airliner like the Boeing 737. It could carry a crew of up to seven into Earth's orbit.

Remote

Flight deck

Liquid oxygen tank

Thrusters

1.

The launch

The shuttle blasted off using the orbiter's main engines and two solid rocket boosters (**1**). Two minutes later, at a height of 28 miles (45 km), the boosters would fall away (**2**). They would land in the Atlantic Ocean by parachute. Ships collected them so that they could be refueled for another flight. At a height of 70 miles (113 km), 8.5 minutes into the mission, the almost-empty external tank (**3**) would fall into the Indian Ocean.

Liquid hydrogen tank

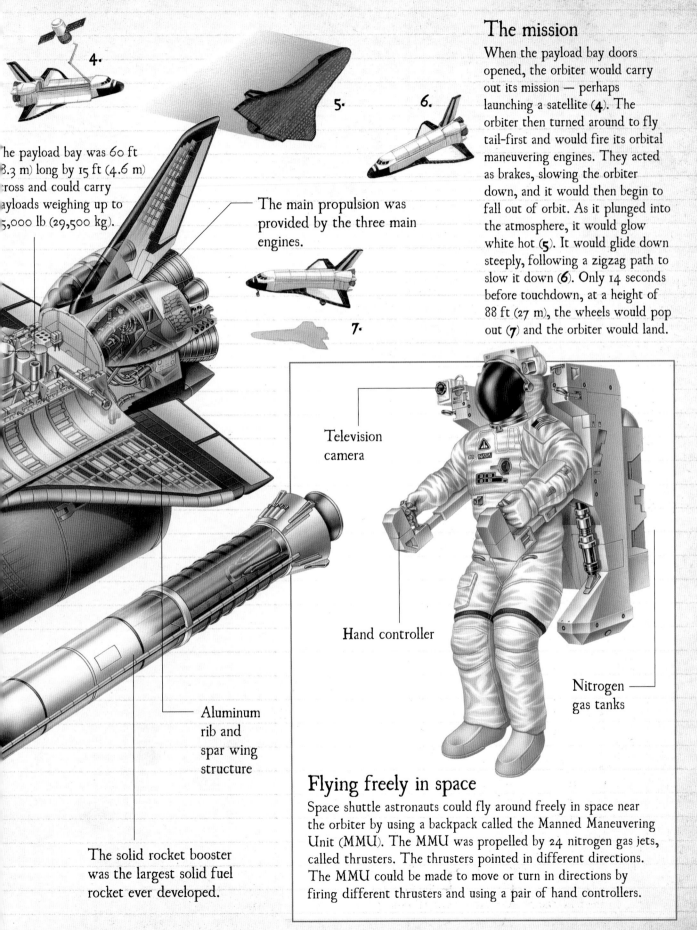

4.

5.

6.

7.

The payload bay was 60 ft (18.3 m) long by 15 ft (4.6 m) across and could carry payloads weighing up to 65,000 lb (29,500 kg).

The main propulsion was provided by the three main engines.

The mission

When the payload bay doors opened, the orbiter would carry out its mission — perhaps launching a satellite (**4**). The orbiter then turned around to fly tail-first and would fire its orbital maneuvering engines. They acted as brakes, slowing the orbiter down, and it would then begin to fall out of orbit. As it plunged into the atmosphere, it would glow white hot (**5**). It would glide down steeply, following a zigzag path to slow it down (**6**). Only 14 seconds before touchdown, at a height of 88 ft (27 m), the wheels would pop out (**7**) and the orbiter would land.

Television camera

Hand controller

Nitrogen gas tanks

Aluminum rib and spar wing structure

The solid rocket booster was the largest solid fuel rocket ever developed.

Flying freely in space

Space shuttle astronauts could fly around freely in space near the orbiter by using a backpack called the Manned Maneuvering Unit (MMU). The MMU was propelled by 24 nitrogen gas jets, called thrusters. The thrusters pointed in different directions. The MMU could be made to move or turn in directions by firing different thrusters and using a pair of hand controllers.

Space stations

A space station is a large craft that stays in space for several months or years, and is visited by different crews. Docking ports allow spacecraft to dock (connect) with the station. Early space stations were launched complete, but larger modern space stations are now launched in pieces and assembled in space. These craft let scientists carry out long-term experiments and observations, for example, to study the effects of long space missions on the human body, which will be very important should we one day send people to the planets.

Salyut 1

The first space station, *Salyut* (Russian for "salute") 1, was launched on April 19, 1971, into an orbit 124 miles (200 km) above the Earth. Two *Soyuz* crews (see page 137) visited the craft before it re-entered the atmosphere on October 11, 1971, and burned up. *Salyut* 1 carried two telescopes for observing the stars. The cosmonauts carried out medical experiments on each other and studied how plants grow in space.

Country: Russia
Date: 1971
Size: 42 ¾ ft (13 m)
Construction: aluminum, steel
Top speed: 17,500 mph (28,000 km/h)
On board: Up to 5 crew

Skylab

Skylab was the first American space station. It was made from an empty fuel tank from a *Saturn* rocket (see page 137). Severe vibration during launch tore off a shield and solar panel, but *Skylab* survived. Three crews, each with three astronauts, spent 171 days inside it. They took 182,000 photographs of the Sun, 40,000 of the Earth, and 2,500 of the comet Kohoutek. They also carried out many scientific experiments. The abandoned *Skylab* crashed to Earth in July 1979.

Country: U.S.
Date: 1973
Size: 84 ft (25.6 m)
Construction: aluminum, steel
Top speed: 17,500 mph (28,000 km/h)
On board: 3 crew

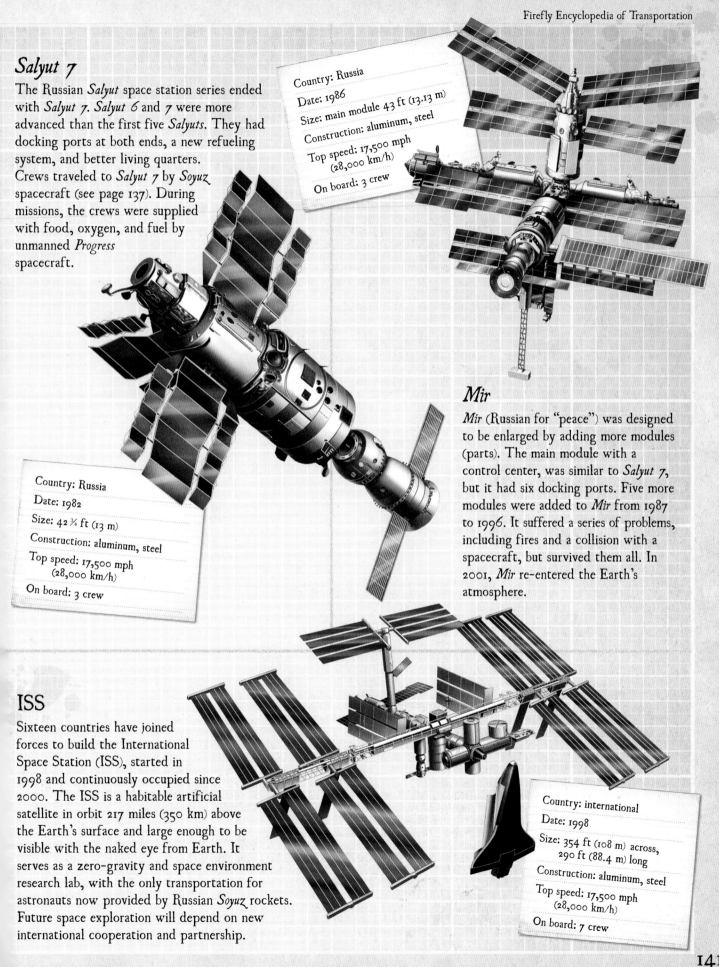

Salyut 7

The Russian *Salyut* space station series ended with *Salyut 7*. *Salyut 6* and *7* were more advanced than the first five *Salyuts*. They had docking ports at both ends, a new refueling system, and better living quarters. Crews traveled to *Salyut 7* by *Soyuz* spacecraft (see page 137). During missions, the crews were supplied with food, oxygen, and fuel by unmanned *Progress* spacecraft.

Country: Russia
Date: 1986
Size: main module 43 ft (13.13 m)
Construction: aluminum, steel
Top speed: 17,500 mph (28,000 km/h)
On board: 3 crew

Country: Russia
Date: 1982
Size: 42 ¾ ft (13 m)
Construction: aluminum, steel
Top speed: 17,500 mph (28,000 km/h)
On board: 3 crew

Mir

Mir (Russian for "peace") was designed to be enlarged by adding more modules (parts). The main module with a control center, was similar to *Salyut 7*, but it had six docking ports. Five more modules were added to *Mir* from 1987 to 1996. It suffered a series of problems, including fires and a collision with a spacecraft, but survived them all. In 2001, *Mir* re-entered the Earth's atmosphere.

ISS

Sixteen countries have joined forces to build the International Space Station (ISS), started in 1998 and continuously occupied since 2000. The ISS is a habitable artificial satellite in orbit 217 miles (350 km) above the Earth's surface and large enough to be visible with the naked eye from Earth. It serves as a zero-gravity and space environment research lab, with the only transportation for astronauts now provided by Russian *Soyuz* rockets. Future space exploration will depend on new international cooperation and partnership.

Country: international
Date: 1998
Size: 354 ft (108 m) across, 290 ft (88.4 m) long
Construction: aluminum, steel
Top speed: 17,500 mph (28,000 km/h)
On board: 7 crew

Into the unknown

Transportation in the most remote places and in extreme conditions calls for extraordinary vehicles. Deep-sea explorers travel inside a thick metal sphere that protects them from the crushing water pressure. Scientists who work in the icy polar regions use tracked vehicles to travel across snow. The tracks spread the vehicle's weight and help to stop it from sinking into the snow. The remotest places of all, other worlds, are explored by robot vehicles. They have driven across the Moon and Mars, guided by drivers on Earth linked to the vehicles by radio.

Mathematician David Bushnell's *Turtle* (1776) was a forerunner of the modern submarine. It only carried one man, who had to crank the propeller by hand, adjust the water ballast (weight), and steer with very tiny portholes to peer through.

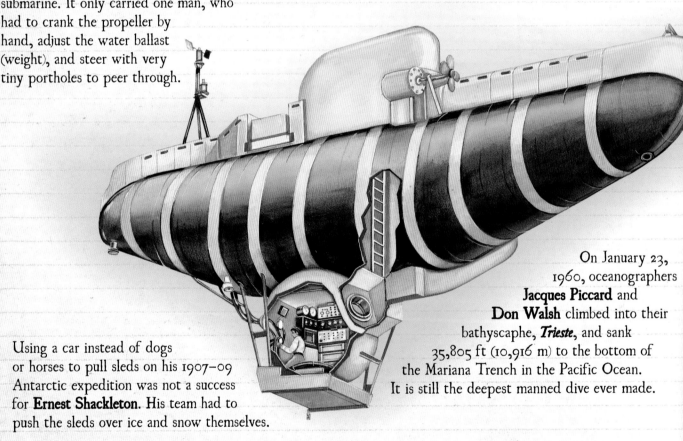

On January 23, 1960, oceanographers **Jacques Piccard** and **Don Walsh** climbed into their bathyscaphe, *Trieste*, and sank 35,805 ft (10,916 m) to the bottom of the Mariana Trench in the Pacific Ocean. It is still the deepest manned dive ever made.

Using a car instead of dogs or horses to pull sleds on his 1907–09 Antarctic expedition was not a success for **Ernest Shackleton**. His team had to push the sleds over ice and snow themselves.

In 1997, the **Sojourner rover** spent 85 days exploring the surface of Mars, studying rocks until its power source failed.

Although humans have never landed on Mars, we have sent rovers to explore its surface. The **Opportunity rover** has been working on Mars since it landed in 2004, while *Curiosity*, a rover the size of a small car, landed on the planet in 2012. Perhaps, in the future, humans will be able to travel to Mars too.

The crews of *Apollo 15, 16,* and *17* took an electric car, the **Apollo lunar rover**, to the Moon to travel farther across the surface than earlier astronauts.

Timeline

DATE	EVENT
BC	
10,000	In different parts of the world, people begin to travel on water. They make rafts by fixing several logs together, or hollow out tree trunks to make dugout canoes.
5000	In western Asia, people begin to tame animals for farming. They use creatures such as the ox and ass to help them carry heavy loads.
3500	The wheel is invented in Mesopotamia (modern Iraq). Made of solid wooden planks, the first wheels are fitted to a framework to make a simple cart.
3000	Mesopotamian people introduce the yoke, a shoulder-board that enables oxen to pull vehicles such as carts.
3000	The world's first sailing boats are built in Egypt. They are used for transportation along the Nile River.
2000	Southeast Asian people build double canoes with sails. They travel across the Pacific, founding the first communities of the Polynesian islands.
1900	Long-distance roads begin to be built in Europe for walking or marching.
1200	Seafarers from Phoenicia (eastern Mediterranean) begin to use the stars for navigation.
1000	The first kites are built in China. Some are so large that they can carry a person.
800	The Phoenicians build the first biremes, warships with two banks of oars, which become the fastest ships.
550	The ancient Greeks introduce four-horse racing chariots.
500	The Silk Road, a route from China to Persia (Iran), is established. Merchants bring spices and other goods.
200	The first ships with lateen (triangular) sails travel along the Mediterranean.
AD	
100	The stirrup and padded saddle are invented in China, making horses easier to ride; at the same time, the padded horse collar helps horses pull heavy carts.
100	Chinese shipbuilders introduce the stern rudder to replace the long steering oar.
400	Straight roads stretch across the vast Roman empire, providing the world's first organized transportation network.
850	The Vikings develop sailing ships in which they travel along Europe's coasts and rivers. They design sleek longships for warfare and broader, slower boats for trading.
1040	Chinese scientists create gunpowder that can be used to power rockets.
1120	Chinese sailors are the first to use a magnetic compass for navigation.
1250	Broad, single-masted sailing ships called cogs are built in Europe. They are used for carrying cargo and as warships.
1400	Wagon-builders find a way of using leather straps to hang a vehicle's body from the framework, or chassis. They create the first suspension system.
1400	The carrack, a compact, three-masted vessel, appears in Europe and soon begins to replace the cog.
1505	Italian artist Leonardo da Vinci draws a flying machine with flapping wings. His notebooks also contain sketches of a never-built helicopter and a parachute.
1550	The galleon, a high-sided sailing ship, dominates in Europe for trade and warfare.
1620	Dutchman Cornelius Drebbel builds a submarine, which is tested under the River Thames in London. The trials are successful, but the vessel does not catch on.
1662	The first organized, horse-drawn bus service begins in Paris.
1710	Using gears and pulleys, shipbuilders figure out how to link a rudder to a wheel for steering.

Thousands of years ago, Pacific island fishing boats used outriggers (balancing floats) to keep upright against the currents and winds.

Galleons were tall, elegant fighting ships, which carried rows of cannons. This extra weight made the ships unstable, but the inward sloping sides of the ship kept it steady.

French brothers Joseph Michel and Jacques Etienne Montgolfier made the first manned flight in a hot-air balloon heated by a fire of straw, in 1783.

1717 British astronomer Edmond Halley designs a diving bell.

1730 "Wagonways" are built in Europe. With their metal tracks for the wagon wheels, they are the ancestors of the later railways.

1750s Stagecoach services are in regular operation in the U.S. and Europe.

1759 British clockmaker John Harrison wins a prize for the first clock to keep accurate time at sea. It is now possible to work out longitude, so ocean sailors can tell exactly where they are for the first time.

1769 French engineer Nicholas Cugnot builds his steam carriage, the world's first steam-powered vehicle.

1783 The French Montgolfier brothers build a hot-air balloon and launch it on its first flight. Another Frenchman, Sebastien Lenormand, makes parachute drops from a tree.

1784 William Murdock, assistant to the Scottish engineer James Watt, builds and tests his steam-powered tricycle.

1784 The first mail coach service begins. It goes from London to Bath.

1804 British engineer Richard Trevithick builds the world's first steam railway engine.

1807 The *Clermont*, built by Robert Fulton, is the first reliable steamboat. It travels up and down the Hudson River.

1816 Scotsman John McAdam starts work on improving road surfaces.

1829 Stephenson's *Rocket* wins the Rainhill Trials to become the first all-around most practical railway engine.

1832 Horse-drawn trams begin a new form of inner-city transportation in New York City.

1838 The steamship *Sirius* becomes the first vessel to cross the Atlantic Ocean under its own power.

1852 Frenchman Henri Giffard flies the first steam airship.

1859 Ironclads, warships whose wooden hulls are protected by iron plates, are introduced. The first is the French vessel, *La Gloire*.

1859 Frenchman Etienne Lenoir builds the first internal combustion engine. It is powered by gas.

1863 The first underground railway, with steam locomotives, opens in London.

1869 The Central Pacific and Union Pacific Railroads meet to form the first coast-to-coast railway in the U.S.

1879 The first electric railway is built in Berlin, Germany.

1883 The Orient Express train service begins to carry passengers between Paris and Constantinople (modern Istanbul), Turkey.

1885 Carl Benz, a German engineer, builds the world's first gasoline-driven car.

1885 The British Rover safety bicycle is the first with equal-sized wheels and a chain drive.

1892 German engineer Rudolf Diesel patents a new form of engine that will be named after him.

1897 Turbinia, a small turbine-driven steam vessel, breaks speed records. Soon many ships will be powered by turbines.

1903 The Wright brothers make the first powered flights in their airplane, *The Flyer,* at Kitty Hawk, North Carolina.

1908 The Model T Ford, the most successful of the early mass-produced cars, begins production in the U.S.

1910 The first seaplane is built by French engineer Henri Fabre.

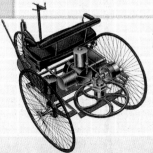

Karl Benz drove the first motorized tricycle in 1885 at the speed of a trotting horse.

The Volkswagen Beetle ("people's wagon") was designed by Dr. Ferdinand Porsche in 1936. Since then, over 20 million of these cars have been sold in 30 countries.

Timeline

DATE	EVENT
1912	The world's largest liner, *Titanic*, sinks on her maiden voyage when it hits an iceberg.
1914	The Atlantic and Pacific oceans are linked with the opening of the Panama Canal.
1919	British flyers John Alcock and Arthur Whitten-Brown make the first nonstop flight across the Atlantic.
1920	The first aircraft with a retracting undercarriage, the Dayton-Wright RB monoplane, is produced.
1923	Aircraft carriers are built for the British and Japanese navies.
1929	Synchromesh, a new design feature on a gearbox, is introduced by the General Motors Corporation. It makes gear-changing much easier.
1933	With the 247, the Boeing Corporation introduces the first modern airliner.
1936	The Volkswagen Beetle, the first "people's car," is designed.
1937	British inventor Frank Whittle builds the world's first jet engine.
1939	The first practical helicopter is designed by Igor Sikorsky.
1947	The American Bell X-1 rocket plane becomes the first vehicle to break the sound barrier.
1952	The De Havilland Company introduces the Comet, the first jet airliner.
1955	The first nuclear-powered submarine, the American *Nautilus*, enters service.
1957	Russia launches *Sputnik 1*, the first artificial satellite to orbit the Earth.
1959	The Austin Mini goes on the market.
1959	The first practical hovercraft is demonstrated.
1961	The Soviet spacecraft *Vostok 1* carries cosmonaut Yuri Gagarin, the first human to travel into space.
1964	Super-fast "bullet trains" begin to transform travel in Japan.
1969	The American spacecraft *Apollo 11* takes the first astronauts to the Moon.
1969	Concorde, the supersonic airliner makes its first test flight.
1969	The Boeing 747, or jumbo jet, flies for the first time.
1970	*Salyut 1*, the first space station, is orbiting the Earth.
1976	Two unmanned *Viking* spacecraft land on Mars.
1981	The space shuttle *Columbia* makes its first flight.
1981	French high-speed train, the TGV, starts to carry passengers.
1989	The American stealth bomber, the Northrop B-2, flies for the first time.
1994	The Channel Tunnel opens, linking Britain and France by rail.
1997	Toyota Prius is the first mass-produced gas-electric hybrid car.
2001	Space station *Mir* re-enters Earth's atmosphere after 15 years in orbit.
2004	Shanghai Airport Maglev line opens in China, becoming the world's fastest commercial rail service, traveling at up to 270 mph (430 km/h).
2010	Launch of Nissan Leaf, the first commercially available plug-in electric car, with 200,000 sold by 2015.
2012	Turanor PlanetSolar, the world's largest solar-powered boat, becomes the first to circumnavigate the globe.
2015	Toyota Mirai is the first commercially available hydrogen fuel cell car.
2015	First fully self-driven ride on public roads is completed by a Google car in Austin, Texas.

Sputnik 1 is launched in 1957 and the "space race" begins.

The Japanese Shinkansen, or Bullet Train, has a maximum service speed of 137 mph (220 km/h).

The Titanic was the largest ship of its time. But on its maiden voyage in 1912 it hit an iceberg and sank in the Atlantic Ocean.

Transportation trailblazers

The De Havilland Comet was the world's first jet airliner. Passengers loved it because it flew higher and faster than any other.

rmstrong, Neil, American astronaut (1930–2012) Born in Ohio, rmstrong was a pilot and test pilot efore being selected as an astronaut in 962. On July 20, 1969, he was the first erson to land on the Moon, speaking the mous words, "That's one small step for a] man, one giant leap for mankind."

eebe, Charles, American naturalist nd explorer (1877–1962) Beebe was n expert on birds who was also terested in exploring under the sea. ogether with engineer Otis Barton, he reated the bathysphere, a spherical diving essel which they took to the record epth of 3,028 ft (923 m).

enz, Karl, German engineer 1844–1929) Benz built the world's first asoline-driven motor car, which took to e road in 1885.

ériot, Louis, French aviator 1872–1936) Blériot made the first flight cross the English Channel on July 25, 909. He flew a 24-horsepower onoplane that he had built himself.

raun, Wernher von, German-merican rocket scientist (1912–77) orn in Germany, Wernher von Braun eveloped the V-2 rocket weapons used uring World War II. After the war, he noved to the U.S., where he worked on e rockets for the first Earth satellites nd on the Saturn rockets used for the pollo moon landing.

ampbell, Donald, British racing river (1921–67) Campbell set several peed records, both on land and on the vater, following his father's land-speed ecord of 174 mph (280 km/h) in 1927. ampbell died on Coniston Water in England during his attempt to be the first person to travel at over 483 km/h (300 mph)

on water. His own son Donald Wales broke the British land speed record for electric vehicles in 2000 with a speed of 128 mph (205 km/h).

Cayley, George, British scientist (1773–1857) One of the earliest pioneers of aeronautics, Cayley created the first practical glider to carry a person. He realized that powered flight would have to wait until a light but powerful engine could be built.

Cierva, Juan de la, Spanish engineer (1895–1936) Fascinated by flying from an early age, Cierva used his engineering skills to invent and build the autogiro, a forerunner of the helicopter that has both a rotor and an airplane propeller.

Cockerell, Christopher, British inventor (1910–2000) Cockerell worked on radar in World War II, but is famous for inventing the hovercraft, a vehicle that rides on a cushion of air. Cockerell had made a working model hovercraft by 1955. Four years later, a hovercraft was crossing the English Channel.

Cook, James, British explorer (1728–79) One of the greatest navigators of all time, Cook traveled to the Pacific, sailing along the coasts of Australia, New Zealand, and many Pacific islands. He also discovered how to keep people healthy on long voyages. By feeding fresh fruit to his crew, he kept them clear of scurvy, a disease that had plagued sailors for centuries.

Cugnot, Nicholas, French military engineer (1725–1804) Responding to the needs of the army, Cugnot invented a three-wheeled gun carriage that was the first practical steam-driven vehicle. Its top speed was only 2 mph (3.2 km/h), so it did not catch on, and Cugnot had no money to build an improved version.

Daimler, Gottlieb, German inventor (1834–1900) Daimler built a number of improved gas engines before starting work on powered vehicles. In the 1880s, he built very early motor cars and motorcycles.

De Havilland, Geoffrey, British aircraft designer (1882–1965) After building his first aircraft himself in 1908, De Havilland ran a company that came up with some of the most successful aircraft of the time. Its 48-seater jet airliner, the Comet, was the first of its type, and helped bring about long-distance mass air travel.

Diesel, Rudolf, German engineer (1858–1913) During the 1880s, Rudolf Diesel began work to produce a more efficient internal combustion engine. He came up with a design in which the fuel ignites at high pressure and which is still widely used in trucks, buses, and cars. This type of engine is known as the diesel engine.

Dunlop, John Boyd, Scottish inventor (1840–1921) A Scottish vet working in Belfast, Dunlop fitted his son's tricycle with air-filled rubber tires in 1887. In doing this, he was reinventing an earlier idea. Dunlop went on to make money from his tires, founding the Dunlop Rubber Company to make air-filled tires.

The first modern-looking bicycles, such as the Rover, with chains, spokes and equal-sized inflatable tires, appeared in 1885.

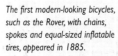

The Saturn V rocket powered the first astronauts to the Moon.

The Hindenburg Zeppelin wa[s] built to carry passengers bet[ween] Germany and Austr[ia in] great luxu[ry]

Farman, Henri, French aviator (1874–1958) Farman was one of the first men to fly, piloting the first Voisin biplane in 1908. He then went into business to build biplanes, and in 1917 made the Goliath bomber, which was converted in 1919 to one of the first airliners.

Ford, Henry, American car manufacturer (1863–1947) Beginning by making cars himself, Ford founded the Ford Motor Company in 1903. Five years later, he was producing the Model T, the first successful mass-produced car. In all, 15 million Model Ts were made, bringing motoring within the reach of ordinary Americans.

Fulton, Robert, American inventor (1765–1815) Trained as a painter, Fulton became an engineer during the 1790s. His many inventions included a machine for cutting and polishing marble and a submarine torpedo boat. He is most famous as a pioneer of the steamboat. His vessel *Clermont*, launched on New York's Hudson River in 1806, was the first successful steamer.

Gagarin, Yuri, Russian (Soviet) cosmonaut (1934–68) Gagarin was the first man in space. He orbited the Earth in his spaceship, *Vostok*, in 1961, returning to Earth a Russian hero.

Goddard, Robert, American physicist (1882–1945) One of the greatest pioneers of rocketry, Goddard was little known in his lifetime. He developed the liquid-fuel rocket, built rockets capable of greater and greater speeds, and invented methods of controlling them as they flew. Only after his death was his work recognized.

Goodyear, Charles, American inventor (1800–60) Charles Goodyear spent some 10 years of his life researching and experimenting with rubber. His most important achievement was the invention of vulcanizing (toughening rubber by curing with sulfur), without which road vehicle tires would not have been practical.

Harrison, John, British clockmaker (1693–1776) In 1713, the British government offered a prize for the person who came up with an accurate method of working out longitude at sea. To do this, you need to be able to tell the time, and Harrison set himself the difficult task of making a clock that would be accurate on board ship. He created a series of highly accurate clocks that finally enabled sailors to work out exactly where they were, and, after years of effort, was awarded the prize.

Henry the Navigator, Prince of Portugal (1394–1460) Prince Henry founded a navigation school, set up an observatory, and sent ships across the seas on voyages of exploration. His work paved the way for a great age of sea voyages, during which explorers from Europe were some of the first to visit Africa and America.

Issigonis, Alec, British car designer (1906–88) Born in Turkey, Issigonis moved to Britain in his teens. His most famous design was the Mini, which appeared in 1959 and transformed small cars all over the world.

Johnson, Amy, British aviator (1903–41) Amy Johnson was one of the first women to learn to fly. She made many long-distance flights, most famously from England to Australia in 1930.

Jouffroy d'Abbas, Claude, French inventor (1751–1832) The French nobleman Claude Jouffroy d'Abbas built the first really practical steamboat in 1783. However, his work was ignored until steamboats were taken up by inventors like Robert Fulton.

Lenoir, Étienne, French engineer (1822–1900) The internal combustion engine was invented by French engineer Étienne Lenoir. Lenoir's original engine was fueled by coal gas, but later versions were used in gasoline-powered cars and airplanes.

Lilienthal, Otto, German inventor (1849–96) Lilienthal was a great pioneer of the glider and made many flights in craft that he built himself. He studied the flight of birds, hoping to build a flying machine with flapping wings. Lilienthal fell to his death during one of his flights.

McAdam, John, Scottish engineer (1756–1836) McAdam had a career in business in the U.S. before settling back in Scotland to invent a better way of building roads. He developed a hard-wearing road surface using gravel and crushed stone, and raised them so that they drained properly. The word "tarmac" is derived from this inventor's name.

Messerschmidt, Willy, German aircraft manufacturer (1898–1978) During the mid-20th century, Messerschmidt's company produced aircraft such as the Me.109, the fastest airplane in the world in 1939, and the Me.262, the first jet aircraft to fly in World War II.

The Model T Ford introduced machine-made cars to the masses for the first time. Between 1908 and 1927, more than 15 million Model Ts were made.

The classic Mini was one of the most popular cars ever produced and a total of about 5,387,862 were built until it stopped production in the year 2000.

The modern helicopter design wa[s] developed in the 1930s by Igor Sikorsky, with his VS-300 helicopt[er] first taking flight in 1939.

Montgolfier brothers, French balloonists Joseph Michel (1740–1810) and Jacques Étienne Montgolfier (1745–99) These brothers constructed the first hot-air balloon in 1782. In 1783, they launched the first manned balloon flight, taking two of their friends some 3,000 ft (915 m) high.

Olds, Ransom, American car manufacturer (1864–1950) After trying steam-powered cars, Ransom Olds began to make gasoline-driven Oldsmobiles in 1899. Later he pioneered the assembly-line method of production, which was taken up even more successfully by Henry Ford.

Otto, Nikolaus, German engineer (1832–91) Otto was a pioneer of the internal combustion engine. He invented the four-stroke cycle, the principle still used in car engines today.

Parsons, Charles, Irish engineer (1854–1931) After training as an engineer, Parsons developed the high-speed steam turbine, a device that transformed ship propulsion and electricity generation. He first became famous when his turbine-driven steamship, the *Turbinia*, broke all speed records.

Plimsoll, Samuel, British politician (1824–98) A member of the British Parliament, Samuel Plimsoll was concerned about the safety of overloaded merchant ships that sat too low in the water. He introduced a mark, which was painted on the hull of every merchant ship, showing the point down to which the ship could be loaded. This mark is still called the Plimsoll line.

Porsche, Ferdinand, German car designer (1875–1951) Porsche began as a designer for German companies such as Daimler before he went on to design the famous Volkswagen Beetle, and later the Porsche sports car.

Pullman, George, American businessman (1831–97) The luxurious Pullman sleeping car was patented in 1864 and 1865, after which George Pullman founded a company to produce and sell his invention. Pullman also invented the railway dining car and devised a way of connecting railway coaches with covered passages.

Royce, Henry, British engineer (1863–1933) Royce was an electrical engineer who became interested in cars. He made his first car in 1904 and his work so impressed Charles Rolls (1877–1910) that they joined to form Rolls-Royce, making luxury cars and aircraft engines.

Sikorsky, Igor, Russian-American engineer (1889–1972) While a young man, Sikorsky wanted to produce a craft that could take off vertically, so he came up with the idea of the helicopter, with its spinning rotor. He made his first successful helicopter in 1939 and all later helicopters have been based on this design.

Stephenson, George (1781–1848) and his son Robert (1803–59), British engineers George and Robert were important railway pioneers. They worked together on the Stockton and Darlington and Liverpool and Manchester railways, and on the famous locomotive, the *Rocket*, which set new standards for both speed and reliability.

Tereshkova, Valentina, Russian (Soviet) cosmonaut (1937–) The first woman to fly in space, Valentina Tereshkova piloted the spacecraft *Vostok 6* in 1963. She completed 48 Earth orbits in her three-day flight.

The world's first controlled, powered airplane flight took place in 1903, in a plane built by the American Wright brothers.

Trevithick, Richard, British engineer (1771–1833) Richard Trevithick worked as a mining engineer and made several steam road vehicles before building the first steam railway locomotives.

Westinghouse, George, American inventor (1846–1914) Among Westinghouse's many inventions in the field of engineering, the most famous was the air brake. This allowed a train driver to control the brakes on all the train's carriages at once. This made trains safer and able to go at higher speeds.

Whittle, Frank, British engineer (1907–96) While a student, Whittle began the research which led to the jet engine. His work was ignored by the authorities, but he carried on, patenting his first jet engine in 1930. By 1941, a British jet-powered aircraft, a Gloster E28/39, was in the air.

Wright, Orville (1871–1948) and Wilbur (1867–1912), American pioneers of flying The Wright brothers made the first powered flight ever, in their own-designed glider.

Zeppelin, Count Ferdinand von, German airship manufacturer (1838–1917) Zeppelin was an army officer who became interested in flight. He made his first airship in 1900. Soon, whenever people thought of airships, they thought of Zeppelin.

George and Robert Stephenson's Rocket is the first express passenger locomotive reaching a speed of 29 mph (47 km/h).

Record breakers

The McLaren F1 LM has a top speed of 225 mph (362 km/h) and is considered the fastest incarnation of the McLaren F1 road cars.

On Wheels

First car
The first gasoline-engine car was built by Karl Benz of Mannheim, Germany, in 1885 (see page 14). It was a three-wheeler and could travel at about 8 mph (13 km/h).

Most popular cars
The first really popular car was the Model T Ford (see page 20), which was made from 1908 to 1927. In that time around 15 million Model Ts were made. They are still being driven today by car enthusiasts. But more Volkswagen Beetles (see page 20) were produced than any other type of car. When production in Germany stopped in the early 1970s, there were over 16 million Beetles.

Most economical vehicle
Probably the best fuel consumption figures to date were achieved by a vehicle designed by Honda during a contest in Finland in 1996. The Honda managed 9,426 mpg (3,336 km/liter) — 250 times better than many standard family cars.

Fastest car
The world's fastest car is *Thrust SSC* (see page 16), which is powered by two jet engines. *Thrust SSC*, driven by Andy Green of Britain, was the first car to go faster than the speed of sound.

Fastest racecar
The racecars that travel fastest are drag racers (see page 16), which move from standing to speeds of over 310 mph (500 km/h) on a course of just 1,320 ft (402 m). The world record was set by American driver Gary Scelzi, who reached 326 1/2 mph (522.3 km/h) in 1998.

Fastest production car
The McLaren F1 is the fastest car that can be driven on the road. It is capable of speeds of up to 240 mph (386.7 km/h) and can accelerate from 0 to 60 mph (96 km/h) in a little over three seconds.

Longest car
People often try to build cars that are long enough to beat the world record. These machines are so long that they are not practical road-going vehicles — but they make interesting displays at fairs and exhibitions. Probably the longest to date measures 100 ft (30.5 m) and was designed by Jay Ohrberg. The American vehicle has 24 wheels and there is a small swimming pool, complete with a diving board, in the rear.

Longest bicycle
The longest modern bicycle was made during the 1980s, measuring 73 ft (22.2 m) long, and was ridden by four people. But in the late 19th century, a 10-person bicycle called La Décuplette was built in France.

Fastest cyclist
Some cyclists have traveled faster than most people have ever managed in a car. This is because a cycle can pick up speed when traveling in the slipstream of another powered vehicle. The fastest to date was the Dutch cyclist Fred Rompelberg, who clocked up an amazing 167 mph (268.8 km/h) in 1995.

On Water

First around the world
Portuguese navigator Ferdinand Magellan embarked with five ships to sail around the world in 1519. During the journey, Magellan and most of his crew of 260 men died, but in 1522 one of his ships with 18 aboard completed the voyage.

First across the Atlantic
The first likely sailors to have crossed the Atlantic were Viking seamen in around 1001. This was the year when Leif the Lucky, son of Erik the Red, first set foot on the country he called Vinland, which was probably Newfoundland, Canada.

Fastest under sail
The swiftest sailing vessel is the *Yellow Pages Endeavour*, a trimaran with three short hulls and a sail that is 40 ft (12 m) high. In 1993, the vessel managed a speed of 46 1/2 knots (86.2 km/h) at Sandy Point, Australia.

First submarine strike
The *Hunley*, a Confederate submarine, sunk a Union sloop in 1864, during the American Civil War (1861–65). It rammed a torpedo attached to a harpoon-like bow into the enemy's wooden hull, released a 150-ft (45 m) rope, withdrew and then tightened the rope to activate the explosive. It was not until World War I (1914–18) that another submarine sank a ship in battle.

Water speed record
The hydroplane *Spirit of Australia* set the water speed record in 1978. The craft, driven by Ken Warby, reached a speed of 276 knots (511.1 km/h). However, Warby accelerated to about 300 knots (555 km/h) on another occasion the previous year, but officials were not present to witness the record.

Biggest warships

The world's largest warships are aircraft carriers owned by the U.S. Navy. They are seven Nimitz Class carriers, the biggest of which are 333 m (1,092 ft) long. These vast floating runways can carry almost 100 aircraft.

Biggest submarines

The largest submarines ever built belonged to the Russian Typhoon class. Typhoons are 172 m (563 ft) in length, are powered by twin nuclear reactors and can travel at 46 km/h (25 knots) when submerged.

Biggest cargo ships

The *Jahre Viking* of Norway is the world's largest ship. The vessel is a supertanker and is 458 m (1,503 ft) in length and 69 m (226 ft) wide. It takes about five minutes to walk from the bow (front) of the ship to the stern (rear).

Container capacity

Big container ships can carry up to 2,700 separate containers. If you stacked them all one on top of the other, they would reach the height of Mount Everest.

Longest yachts

Abdul Aziz, the yacht of the Saudi Arabian royal family, is 147 m (482 ft) long.

Rowing the Atlantic

In 1997, two New Zealanders, Phil Stubbs and Robert Hamill, rowed across the Atlantic Ocean in 41 days, beating the previous record by 32 days.

The world's largest steam engines were called the "Big Boys." They were built for the Union Pacific Railroad to haul 4,400-ton (4,000 tonne) freight trains through the mountains.

On the Tracks

Largest steam engine

The biggest, heaviest and most powerful steam locomotives in the world are the "Big Boys" (see page 87). The enormous engines weigh around 550 tons (500 tonnes) and were built to pull freight trains across Utah. The locomotives were 13 1/4 ft (40 m) long, and the driving wheel was 5 3/4 ft (1.8 m) in diameter. The firebox alone was large enough for a family dining room.

Fastest steam engine

The British *Mallard* (see page 87), with its sleek streamlined body, is the fastest-ever steam locomotive. In 1938, it reached 126 mph (201 km/h) on a special journey along the main line between London and Edinburgh.

Largest diesel engine

The longest diesel engines run in the U.S. They work on the Union Pacific Railway, are almost 100 ft (30 m) long and weigh 252 tons (229 tonnes).

Largest freight train

Probably the longest ever freight train was made up of 500 coal wagons and ran on Ohio's Norfolk and Western Railroad, in 1967. The train was pulled by six diesel locomotives and was 4 miles (6.4 km) in length.

Longest rail tunnel

The world's longest railway tunnel connects the Japanese islands of Honshu and Hokkaido. The tunnel is 33 miles (53 km) long, and most of it runs under water.

Largest railway station

New York's Grand Central Station is the world's largest. It has 44 platforms.

Widest track

Some of the world's widest trains run on track with a gauge (width) of 5 1/2 ft (1.676 m). This gauge is used in China, India, Pakistan, Spain, Portugal and Argentina.

Fastest modern train

Of the world's various high-speed train services, the current record-holder is a French *TGV* (*Train à Grande Vitesse*). In 1990, the TGV (see page 93) reached 320 mph (515 km/h) near Vendôme. In normal service, however, *TGVs* run more slowly, with speeds averaging 132 mph (212 km/h) along much of the Paris–Lyon route.

In the Air

First transatlantic solo flight

Charles Lindbergh, a pilot from Detroit, Michigan, made the first solo transatlantic flight in 1927. The journey took just 33 hours in Lindbergh's Ryan monoplane, *The Spirit of St. Louis*. The first nonstop transatlantic crossing (from Newfoundland to Ireland) had been achieved by British pilots John Alcock and Arthur Brown in 1919.

Fastest aircraft

The fastest aircraft of all was the Lockheed SR-71 of 1964. Its top speed was 2,193 mph (3,530 km/h) and it was said to be able to fly as high as 98,000 ft (30,000 m).

Record breakers

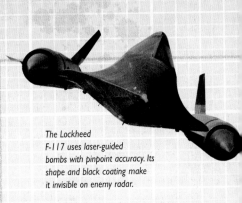

Fastest airliner
The BAC/Aérospatiale Concorde was the world's fastest airliner (see page 119). It reached 1,450 mph (2,333 km/h) — 2.2 times the speed of sound.

Biggest aircraft
The Airbus Super Transport A300-600 Beluga is the world's largest cargo-carrying aircraft. Its vast cargo compartment has a volume of 15,000 sq ft (1,400 sq m) and a length of 124 ft (37.7 m).

Biggest wingspan
The airplane with the longest wingspan was the Hughes H4 Hercules, a flying boat that was also nicknamed the "Spruce Goose." This massive aircraft, which was intended for the U.S. government by American businessman Howard Hughes, had a wingspan of 320 ft (97.5 m). The plane, which cost $40 million to build, was only flown for a single test flight.

Largest airship
The biggest of the great airships was the German hydrogen-filled *Hindenburg*. Completed in March 1936, the *Hindenburg* took 10 days to travel around the world and made some 20 crossings of the Atlantic before it caught fire in May 1937, killing many of those on board.

Smallest airplane
The smallest working, human-piloted airplane was *Bumble Bee Two*. This tiny single-seater was just 9 ft (2.7 m) long and had a wingspan of 5 1/2 ft (1.7 m). The plane, built by Robert Tempe of Arizona, crashed in 1988.

Human-powered flight
In 1979, the first successful human-powered series, the *Gossamer Albatross*, flew across the English Channel. The flight finally fulfilled a dream of human-powered flight that had begun with the first experimental flying machines of the 19th century.

In Space

First living creature in space
The first live creature in space was not a person but a dog. The animal, named Laika, went into space in the Russian *Sputnik 2* in 1957, shortly after the launch of *Sputnik 1*, the first artificial Earth-orbiting satellite.

Shortest space flight
In May 1961, the American astronaut Alan Shepard made the briefest manned space flight on board *Freedom 7*.

The Lockheed F-117 uses laser-guided bombs with pinpoint accuracy. Its shape and black coating make it invisible on enemy radar.

Shepard's spacecraft did not go into orbit, but flew in a huge curve, landing some 15 minutes after it took off. But it did leave the Earth's atmosphere, and made Shepard the second man in space after Russia's Yuri Gagarin.

First space probe on another planet
The Russian probe *Venera 7* was the first space probe to land on another planet. The craft landed on the planet Venus in 1970.

Fastest speed
The fastest-ever speed reached by a human being is 24,791 mph (39,897 km/h). It was achieved by the American astronauts of *Apollo 10* when they returned to Earth in May 1969.

Longest continuous time in space
Russian Valeriy Poliyakov spent 437 days, 17 hours, 58 minutes, and 16 seconds from January 1994 to March 1995 on two *Soyuz* spacecrafts and the space station, *Mir* (see page 141).

A space station is a large craft that stays in space for several months or years. Large modern space stations are now launched in pieces and assembled in space.

Glossary of transportation terms

Accelerator
A control, usually a pedal on a car, that allows you to increase or reduce the speed of the engine.

Aerodynamics
The study of the movement of objects through a gas; in road transportation, usually used to cut down friction and make vehicles more efficient.

Aft
Toward the rear of a vessel or aircraft.

Aileron
Flap on an airplane wing that the pilot can move to cause the aircraft to roll left or right and enter a turn.

Airbag
Safety device in a car, consisting of a bag that inflates with air to provide a cushion for the driver or passengers in a crash.

Air-cushion vehicle
A hovercraft that glides over land or water on a layer of compressed air.

Air brakes
Brakes that work using compressed air, used by trucks and trains.

Airship
Lighter-than-air aircraft with a gas-filled balloon-like envelope, an engine and a steering mechanism.

Alcohol
Used in many rockets as a fuel; and, in Brazil, as an alternative fuel to gasoline to run cars.

Alloy
Substance made by mixing two or more metals to improve strength or hardness.

Amphibious
Capable of traveling both on land and in water.

Articulated
Containing a joint; an articulated truck has its front section joined to the rear by a flexible link that makes it easy to maneuver.

Axle
Rod passing through the center of a wheel, allowing the wheel to turn.

Barge
A flat-bottomed vessel, mainly for carrying freight, used mostly on rivers and canals; also a ceremonial boat.

Barque
Three- or four-masted ship with the mizzen- (rear) mast rigged with sails positioned fore-and-aft and the other masts square-rigged.

Barquentine
Three-masted ship with the main- and mizzen- (rear) masts fore-and-aft rigged, and the fore-mast square rigged.

BHP
See Brake horsepower.

Biplane
Airplane with twin wings, one above the other.

Blimp
Small airship that does not have a rigid frame, often used for advertising.

Boat
Any small watergoing vessel, powered by oars, sails, or motor.

Boiler
Container in which water is boiled to produce steam in a steam engine.

Brake horsepower (BHP)
Unit of measurement of the effective power of an engine, measured by working out the force applied to a brake by the engine drive shaft in a special testing machine (see also Horsepower).

Bridge
Place on a ship from which the captain controls the vessel.

Broadside
All the guns of a ship that can be fired together in the same direction.

Buggy
Lightweight horse-drawn carriage; or small vehicle used for recreation.

Bulkhead
Dividing partition wall inside a ship or aircraft.

Bullet train
Very fast bullet-nosed train as used on the Japanese Shinkansen network.

Cab
Part of a truck or railway engine that accommodates the driver.

Caravel
Light sailing ship used between the 14th and 17th centuries.

Carbon fiber
Very strong, lightweight material used in making many items related to transportation, from turbine blades to high-performance boats.

Cargo
Goods carried by a truck, merchant ship or freight train.

Carrack
Large trading ship used between the 14th and 16th centuries.

Catamaran
Ship or boat with twin hulls.

Chassis
Supporting frame and wheels of a motor vehicle or carriage.

Clipper
Tall-masted cargo-carrying sailing ship of the 19th century, capable of very fast sea journeys.

Cockpit
Part of an aircraft, spacecraft, racecar and powerboat where the captain, pilot or driver sits.

Cog
North European cargo ship of the Middle Ages with a single mast and square sail.

Commuter train
Train used by people traveling to work, usually from the outskirts to the center of a large city.

Composites
Plastics, such as carbon fiber, which are used in vehicle construction. Alloys, which are also used, are metals.

Conning tower
Upward-pointing structure on a submarine used for navigation and as the entrance to the vessel.

Container
A standard-sized steel box used on many ships, trucks and trains for carrying cargo.

Convertible
Car with a roof, often made of fabric, that can be folded back or taken off.

Corsair
Pirate, especially one from North Africa; or the vessel sailed by such a person.

Coupé
Two-door car with a roof that has a marked downward slope toward the back.

Cow-catcher
Structure on the front of a railway locomotive designed to sweep obstructions off the track.

Craft
General term for any ship or boat, or any air or space vehicle.

Crew
Group of people who work on board a ship or aircraft, under the command of the captain.

Cylinder
Tube-shaped part of an engine, in which a piston moves up and down.

Deck
One of the horizontal floors of a ship or aircraft.

Derailleur
Gearing system used on bicycles, in which the chain can be shifted from one drive cog to another.

Diesel engine
Type of internal combustion engine in which the fuel ignites because it is injected directly into the cylinder when the air has been compressed to high pressure.

Dirigible
Craft, usually an airship, that can be steered, rather than just drifting like a free balloon.

Drag
The force that tends to slow down any vehicle traveling through air or water.

Engine
Mechanical device that powers a ship, car, train or other vehicle.

Exhaust
Waste gases produced by an engine. Also, the part of the engine through which the waste emissions pass.

Ferry
Vessel that carries passengers (and often vehicles) back and forth across a stretch of water.

Fiberglass
Lightweight material made by molding a mat or cloth of thin glass fibers in a plastic matrix. Used in some car bodies and the hulls of some boats; also called glass-fiber or GRP (glass-reinforced plastic).

Fore
Toward the front of a vessel or aircraft.

Four-stroke cycle
Most gasoline and diesel engines operate on this cycle of strokes (the up-and-down movements) of the pistons.

Four-wheel drive (4WD)
Type of motor vehicle in which the power of the engine is transfered to all four wheels (rather than the standard two), to provide good traction on difficult ground.

Freight
Cargo or goods. A freighter is a cargo vessel.

Friction
Resistance felt when one surface rubs against another.

Galleon
Large sailing ship with high fore and aftercastles, used in the 15th and 16th centuries.

Gallon
Non-metric measurement of capacity equivalent to approximately 4.5 liters.

Gauge
Measurement of the distance between a pair of railway wheels or rails. This varies around the world: the standard gauge in North America, most of Western Europe and China is 56½ in. (143.5 cm).

Gears
System of cogs that transmits the motion of the engine to the wheels of a motor vehicle and which can change the speed and torque available.

Glider
Aircraft designed in a similar way to an airplane, but without an engine. Very efficient aerodynamic design allows it to stay airborne using natural upcurrents.

Hatchback
Car with a sloping rear door that opens upward.

Haul
To pull, to transport, or (of a ship) to change direction.

Helium
A very light, chemically inert gas often used in airships.

Horsepower (hp)
Measurement of power, roughly equivalent to the strength of one horse.

Hovercraft
Vessel supported by a cushion of air, capable of traveling over land and sea.

HPV (Human Powered Vehicle)
Any human-powered transportation including bicycle-style vehicles.

Hull
Body of a ship.

Hydrofoil
Vessel fitted with winglike structures under the hull called foils that develop lift and raise the hull out of the water as it travels.

Hydrogen
A very light, highly flammable gas that was once used in balloons and airships.

Jet engine
Engine that uses the momentum of a jet of hot exhaust gas to propel an airplane or other vehicle.

Juggernaut
A term (of Hindu origin) now used to describe a very large truck.

Jumbo jet
Large, wide-bodied airliner.

Jump jet
Fighter airplane that can take off and land vertically.

Keel
Main structural part of a ship that stretches along the whole of the bottom of the vessel; it may also protrude down into the water to help make the vessel more stable.

Kilowatt
Unit of power now replacing horsepower in automotive engineering.

Knot
Measurement of speed equivalent to 1 nautical mile per hour (1.853184 km/h).

Lift
Force needed to raise an aircraft into the air.

Liner
Large vessel that carries passengers.

Liter
Standard metric measurement of capacity.

Locomotive
The engine unit of a railway train.

Mach
A measurement of an aircraft's speed compared to the speed of sound. Mach 1 means the plane is traveling at the speed of sound; Mach 2 means twice the speed of sound. At sea level, the speed of sound is 758 mph (1,220 km/h) but it is slower the higher you go.

Machine gun
Automatic gun that can fire many bullets at high speed, attached to tanks, fighter aircraft, bombers and other military vehicles. Also carried by infantry.

Magnet
Piece of iron that attracts other metals containing iron.

Maneuver
Intricate movement of vehicle that requires skill to achieve.

Marshalling yard (or classification yard)
Area containing many linked railway tracks, where railway wagons are sorted and joined together to form trains.

Mass production
Method of making objects in large numbers using standard, repetitive processes, as with the modern motor car.

Mast
Vertical structure or pole that carries a ship's sails, or other equipment in powered vessels.

Merchant ship
Vessel designed to carry goods, particularly from one country to another.

Microlight
Very small, lightweight airplane.

Module
Single part that can be interchanged with other parts of the same size.

Monorail
Railway that travels on a single rail.

Nozzle
Outlet tube or spout; pipe through which fuel enters a cylinder in an internal combustion engine. Also exit zone of jet or rocket engine.

Nuclear power
Power generated as a result of a nuclear reaction. The heat of the nuclear reaction is used to create steam and drive a turbine.

Orbit
Circular path around a planet or moon followed by a spacecraft or satellite, or by one astronomical body around another.

Outrigger
Stabilizing framework or structure sticking out from one side of a boat; or, a boat with such a structure to increase stability.

Oxidizer
Chemical supplied to a rocket engine that helps the fuel to burn.

Paddle
Short oar, normally used in a canoe.

Pantograph
Metal framework fitted on top of an electric locomotive or tram, to collect current from overhead wires.

Piston
Cylindrical component that moves up and down inside the cylinder of an engine.

Pneumatic tire
Vehicle tire filled with compressed air.

Probe
Vehicle used for space exploration; particularly an unmanned vehicle sent to one of the planets or to travel outside the solar system.

Propeller
Device made up of a shaft and several specially shaped blades, used to drive a ship or airplane; also called a screw.

Prototype
The first finished example of a vehicle, built as a one-off, before regular production begins and from which later examples can be copied.

Pullman
Railway carriage with comfortable accommodation for both sitting and for sleeping.

Rack and pinion
Steering mechanism used in many cars, in which a toothed wheel (the pinion) engages with a toothed bar (the rack).

Radar
System that uses reflected radio waves to detect invisible objects, such as aircraft in the sky or ships at sea; it is also used by pilots and sailors to work out their own position. The word radar comes from the phrase "Radio Detection And Ranging."

Reconnaissance
A first survey of an area to learn its features; air forces or navies may use specialized reconnaissance aircraft or ships to check for enemy positions.

Rickshaw
Small carriage with two wheels, pulled by a person or by someone riding a bicycle.

Rig
The arrangement of sails on a boat or ship.

Rigging
The ropes that hold up a ship's masts and control its sails.

Rolling stock
Railway vehicles — including locomotives, carriages and goods wagons.

Rotor
Arrangement of spinning blades fitted to a helicopter.

Rudder
Moveable flap for steering a boat or aircraft.

Rush hour
Time when most people are traveling to and from work, school and so on.

Satellite
Object that orbits a planet.

Schooner
Two-masted ship, with sails rigged fore and aft.

Sedan
An enclosed car with front and rear seats.

Ship
Any large seagoing vessel.

Shunting
Moving railway rolling stock from one line to another.

Skidoo
Vehicle used in snow, with caterpillar tracks at the rear and steerable skis at the front.

Sleigh
Vehicle with sliding runners, usually used to travel across snow, also called a sledge.

Smokestack
Chimney of a steam locomotive.

Solar power
Energy generated using the rays of the sun.

Stacking
System whereby air traffic control keeps planes waiting to land, circling above at fixed heights.

Station wagon
Car with a rear-door opening onto an area behind the seats designed to carry luggage or other goods.

Stratosphere
Part of the atmosphere, beginning from 5 to 10 miles (8 to 16 km) above the Earth's surface.

Streamlined
Designed with a sleek, aerodynamic body, so that drag is kept low.

Submersible
Small submarine used for exploration and other non-military work.

Subway
Underground railway system serving a town or city. Also called metro in Europe.

Supersonic
Faster than the speed of sound.

Suspension
System of springs and other devices that support a vehicle's body on its axles and is designed to cushion those traveling inside from bumps on the ground.

Tailplane
Flat part of an aircraft's tail, designed to make the craft more stable in flight.

Tanker
Vessel or vehicle in which most of the body is made up of large tanks for carrying liquids in bulk.

Tender
Rear part of a steam locomotive, carrying supplies of coal and water.

Thermals
Currents of warm air on which gliders soar.

Thrust
Pushing force produced by a jet engine or rocket that moves the craft forward.

Tiller
Lever used to control a boat's rudder.

Tolls
Barriers with booths collecting payments to use a stretch of road, canal or bridge.

Ton
Imperial measurement of weight close to a metric tonne (1 ton = 0.9072 tonnes).

Torpedo
Self-propelled underwater weapon which explodes when it hits the target.

Tram
Passenger-carrying vehicle that runs along rails on a road.

Transmission
System (consisting of gearbox and clutch) that transfers power from a motor vehicle's engine to its wheels.

Trolley
Device, fitted to a trolleybus, that collects electric power from overhead wires.

Tug
Ship that tows other vessels.

Turbine
Motor that uses a bladed wheel that is turned by the force of water, steam or burning gas.

Turbo (turbocharger)
Type of turbine fitted to a vehicle engine; it supplies air under pressure to the engine's cylinders for better performance.

Turbofan
Jet engine that uses a large fan to increase the thrust at lower speeds suited to civil aircraft.

Turbojet
Gas turbine engine which propels an aircraft by its high-speed exhaust.

Turboprop
Turbine engine which powers a propeller.

Vessel
Any ship, boat or water-borne transportation.

Wagon
Railway truck for carrying freight; or, a four-wheeled horse-drawn vehicle, especially for carrying goods.

Wind tunnel
Device for producing a steady stream of air, used for testing the aerodynamics of cars, aircraft and other vehicles.

Wingspan
Tip-to-tip length of an aircraft's wings.

ndex

Airbus A321-211 (Air France)

Jaguar XK SS

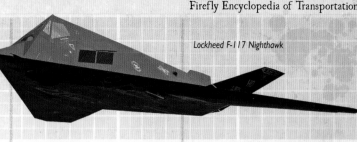

Lockheed F-117 Nighthawk

Acknowledgments

Kinsey & Harrison would like to thank:

John W. Walker, Director at TAL Management Ltd., Hampshire, England (for Cable & Wireless Adventurer); Tim Cley at Reynard Motorsports Ltd., Oxon (for Indy cars); Bart Garbrecht, President at CEO P.R.O.P. Tour, Inc., Lake Hamilton, Florida (for F1 powerboats); Cameron Kellegher at HSBC and Jaguar Racing (for F1 cars); Ford/Pivco Industries AS (forTh!nk car); Pegasus Aviation; Jason Lewis at www.goals.com; Robert Dane and Mark Gold at www.solarsailor.com.

Artwork credits

t = top; b = bottom; l = left; r = right; c = center

Tony Bryan: 38-39; 46-47; 116-17; 118-19; 120-121; 124-125. Peter Bull: 18-19; 52-53; 50-51; 54-55; 56-57; 58-59; 60-61; 64-65; 66-67; 70-71; 72-73; 74-75; 76-77; 82-83; 92-93; 112-113; 114-115; 123 tl; 128 b; 142 c. Nicholas Forder 21 cr, 23 cl, 34, 35, 41 cl, 44, 45, 47 t, c, br, 91 b, 100 b, 104, 105, 106-107, 119 b. Mark Franklin: 12-13; 16-17; 20-21; 28-29; 24-25; 26-27; 30-31; 32-33; 36-37; 40-41; 138-39. John James: 62-63; 134-135 (except tl); 138 l; 139 t. John Lawson: 28-29; 68-69. Simon Roulstone: 14-15; 42-43; 84-85; 86-87; 88-89; 90-91; 94-95; 96-97; 98-99; 100-101; 126-127; 132-133; 134-135; 136-137; 140-141. Peter Sarson: 142tr.

Photographic Credits

t = top; b = bottom; l = left; r = right; c = center

7 NASA; 8 Shutterstock.com; 9 © Niday Picture Library / Alamy Stock Photo; 30 Fifian Iromi/Shutterstock.com; 48 t © Science Museum/Science & Society Picture Library, 48 c Escho/Getty, 48 b Art Konovalov / Shutterstock.com; 49 t Sergei Butorin / Shutterstock.com; 49 c Dyson Industries Ltd, 49 b Resilient Technologies; 50 Ruth Peterkin / Shutterstock.com; 51 Vlada Photo/Shutterstock.com; 69 Chatchai Somwat / Shutterstock.com; 78 tr chrisdorney / Shutterstock.com, 78 cl © Keystone Pictures USA / Alamy Stock Photo, 78 cr © Chris Laurens / Alamy Stock Photo, 78 b Kos Picture Source; 79 t Colin Porteous/Shutterstock.com, 79 bl © paul cox / Alamy Stock Photo, 79 br Seaco Picture Library; 80 i4lcocl2/Shutterstock.com; 81 Peter R Foster IDMA/Shutterstock.com; 92 GuoZhongHua/Shutterstock.com; 102 Science Photo Library/MARTIN BOND; 103 Geert Vanden Wijngaert/AP/Press Association Images; 106 bl Daniel Gale Science Photo Library/MARTIN BOND, 106 br Getty Images/Tim Rue/Bloomberg; 107 Koichi Kamoshida/Getty; 108 tr John S Lander/Getty, 108 c Michal Staniewski, 108 b Getty Images/Brendon Thorne; 109 t Frederic Legrand - COMEO / Shutterstock.com, 109 c Igor Karasi / Shutterstock.com, 109 b Tinxi / Shutterstock.com; 110 motive56 / Shutterstock.com; 111 Piotr Wawrzyniuk / Shutterstock.com; 112 tl rimira, 112 tr © Ericus ‡ Dreamstime.com; 113 tl Sebastian Kaulitzki, 113 tc © Ujang Irwan/Dreamstime.com, 113 tr DnD-Production.com, 113 cr © NG Images / Alamy Stock Photo; 114 ullstein bild/Getty Images; 128t Mikael Damkier, 128 c Stoyan Yotov/Shutterstock.com; 129 t Michael Lee, 129 cl Marco Prati / Shutterstock.com, 129 cr Susan Montgomery / Shutterstock.com, 129 bl Roman Vukolov/Shutterstock.com, 129 br esbobeldijk; 130 Juergen Faelchle; 131 Castleski, 132 © Photo Researchers / Alamy Stock Photo; 138 Jason and Bonnie Grower/Shutterstock.com; 142 Royal Geographical Society (with IBG); 143 tl Popperfoto/NASA, 143 tr NASA, 143 b NASA; 150 Gustavo Fadel/Shutterstock.com; 151 jiawangkun; 152 t Jose Gil; 152 b Andrey Armyagov; 157 Cardinal arrows / Shutterstock.com; 158 urbanbuzz/Shutterstock.com; 159 t Peter Barrett / Shutterstock.com; 159 b NeonLight; 160 Castleski.

Every effort has been made to trace the copyright holders. The publisher apologizes for any unintentional omissions and would be pleased, in such cases, to add an acknowledgement in future editions.

Astronaut on a space mission